media

MANUAL

lighting for video

media

MANUAL

MANUAL

third edition

lighting for video

gerald millerson

ELSEVIER

Focal
Press

AMSTERDAM • BOSTON • HEIDELBERG • LONDON • NEW YORK • OXFORD
PARIS • SAN DIEGO • SAN FRANCISCO • SINGAPORE • SYDNEY • TOKYO
Focal Press is an imprint of Elsevier

Focal Press
An imprint of Elsevier
Linacre House, Jordan Hill, Oxford OX2 8DP
30 Corporate Drive, Burlington, MA 01803

First published as *TV Lighting Methods* 1975
Second edition 1982
Reprinted 1983, 1986, 1987, 1989, 1990
Third edition 1991
Reprinted 1992, 1995, 1996 (twice), 1998, 1999, 2001 (twice), 2003, 2004, 2005

British Library Cataloguing in Publication Data
A catalogue record for this book is available from the British Library

Library of Congress Cataloguing in Publication Data
A catalogue record for this book is available from the Library of Congress

ISBN 0 240 51303 7

For information on all Focal Press publications
visit our website at www.focalpress.com

Working together to grow
libraries in developing countries
www.elsevier.com | www.bookaid.org | www.sabre.org

ELSEVIER   BOOK AID International   Sabre Foundation

Composition by Genesis Typesetting, Laser Quay, Rochester, Kent
Printed and bound in Great Britain by MPG Books Ltd, Bodmin, Cornwall

Contents

Introduction

When *TV Lighting Methods* appeared over a decade ago, it quickly became established as a major primer on TV lighting techniques. Now, to help you get the most from your video camera system, we have revised, extended and re-titled this very practical text to suit your needs today.

Poor lighting can ruin your video! Master the basics of effective lighting, and you take a vital step forward towards successful picture-making.

Persuasive lighting techniques are a subtle blend of practical know-how and artistic anticipation. But many program-makers simply do not have the time or the opportunity to study the craft in depth. That is where *Lighting for Video* can help. It does not assume technical knowledge or previous experience. After covering basics it guides you towards the most effective ways of tackling your particular project; and shows typical professional solutions to everyday situations.

Lighting for Video anticipates your problems. The practices you meet here will enable you to produce top-grade results, whether you are lighting off-the-cuff with a portable compact kit, or tackling a major project with an extensive heavy-duty rig.

It covers techniques that you can apply when using video for training, working on in-house projects, advertising, promotion, sales, etc., in the studio or shooting on location.

You will enjoy lighting. It is a very satisfying, creative experience. If you want to look into the subject in more detail, you will find further study sources listed on page 144.

Acknowledgement

I would like to thank the Director of Engineering of the British Broadcasting Corporation for permission to publish the original title, from which this book is developed.

Gerald Millerson

Why bother?

You can take your video camera most places, and produce pictures. The camera works with the light that is there. If there is not enough, you can usually just open up the lens aperture, or increase the video gain to compensate, or set up lamps near the camera and flood the scene with light. So what's the problem? What are the advantages in knowing about 'lighting techniques'?

To be frank, a lot depends on your circumstances and your standards. Some people are quite satisfied with results that others will find unacceptable. Sometimes you may have little choice, but to accept the lighting conditions as you find them, or make do with an improvized set-up because you do not have the equipment, the time, or the opportunity to improve matters. But in most situations, an understanding of lighting basics will help you to present the subject more effectively, and to achieve higher picture quality.

Random lighting may not be acceptable

There are a number of reasons why you may not be satisfied with just any random lighting for your subject.

Visibility is not enough. A picture should persuade your audience, and hold their attention. A carefully chosen camera viewpoint and well-arranged composition are important, but effective lighting gives a picture *dimension* – depth, solidity, texture, form. The subjects seem to stand out from their surroundings.

Technically, you usually want your pictures to be sharply defined, with good color quality, free from picture-noise ('snow') or other distracting defects. Appropriate lighting helps you achieve higher standards.

Artistically, you want the subjects to appear attractive; lit to reveal (or conceal) particular features. The overall atmosphere should suit the occasion: e.g., high-key surroundings for comedy; mysterious shadowy low-key for dramatic situations. You will want a succession of shots to *match*; avoiding the subject appearing half-lit at one moment, and over-lit the next.

Conditions can vary considerably. Although there will be times when you can shoot in the available light and get excellent results, there is a large element of luck, as you will see! If you are aiming at consistently high standards, and maximum visual appeal, you can't rely on random lighting. You need to assess each situation, and decide the steps needed to get the best out of each shot. That is why professional TV and film units so often go to the trouble of introducing extra lighting, even when shooting in daylight.

TYPICAL LIGHT LEVELS

	Incident light (lux)	Incident light (foot candles)	Typical reflected light level
Bright sunlight	1000,000–50,000	10,000–5,000	6,000–3,000
Hazy sunlight	50,000–25,000	5,000–2,500	3,000–1,500
Bright but cloudy	25,000–20,000	2,500–1,000	1,500–600
Dull, overcast sky	10,000–2,000	1,000–200	600–120
Very dull, evening	2,000–100	200–10	120–6
Sunrise/sunset	100–1	10–0.1	6–0.06
Typical offices	300–200	30–20	18–12
Living room	200–50	20–5	12–3
Corridors, hallways	100–50	10–5	6–3
Well lit streets	20–10	2–1	1.2–0.6
Dimly lit streets	0.1	0.01	

1 foot candle = 10.764 lux   1 lux = 0.0929 foot candles

As a rough approximation, you can estimate from 1 fc = 10 lux. 1/10 lux = 1 fc

Day exteriors
Strong sunlight
Weak sunlight
Sunless sky light
Overcast skies
Evening light
Dawn/dusk/sunset

Day interiors
Large windows
(sunlight, daylight)
Direct onto subject
Reflected onto subject
Small or obscured windows

Daylight augmented with
tungsten/fluorescent lighting

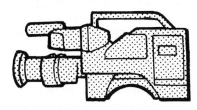

Night interiors
Illuminated ceiling (fluorescent)
Central ceiling light
Pole lamps (standard lamps)
Wall fittings, wall panels
Table lamps
Ceiling spotlights

Firelight
Flashlamp
Candlelight

Night exteriors
Street lighting (strong/weak)
Shop window lighting
Local lighting
Car headlamps
Firelight

AVAILABLE LIGHT

The video camera is able to shoot under a remarkable range of lighting
conditions; although the intensity, quality, direction and contrast may be
very variable

The camera always lies!

There are major differences between the way your eyes see the world around you, and the version interpreted by your video camera. *You* can look around freely, and quickly build up an accurate impression of your surroundings. A *camera* on the other hand, shows only a very limited segment of the scene.

The *flat* image on the screen provides far fewer visual clues to enable you to interpret the scene. If those clues are not clear enough, you may misjudge what you are seeing.

You use perspective clues to form ideas of distance and size, but these can easily become confused in the flat, two-dimensional image.

Your stereoscopic vision, enables you to pick out subjects from their background, and easily assess shape and distance. Features stand out, so that you can for instance, pick out individual trees in a forest scene. On the screen, the same trees are likely to reproduce as a dense merging mass of foliage.

Color helps considerably, to distinguish between various planes. But in a *monochrome* (black-and-white) picture, visual information is very limited, for you have only shades of gray to help form your impressions of the scene. Different hues can reproduce as identical gray values!

The camera's limitations

Eye and brain continually make allowances and adapt to local conditions. So you seem able to detect details in shadowy areas, adjust to varying light intensities, instantaneously refocus.

The video camera can only handle a *limited tonal range*. The maximum contrast it will accept between the brightest and darkest tones is around 20 to 30: a *contrast ratio* of 20:1 to 30:1. Areas in a shot that exceed the maximum (i.e., are over-bright), will crush out to an even white on the screen. Shadow areas and tones that are proportionally too dark, will merge to a detailed black.

Fortunately, you can help to minimize these technical limitations, by systematic lighting techniques, carefully adjusted exposure (*f-stop/lens aperture* adjustment), by appropriate lighting treatment, or good scenic treatment (e.g., repainting surfaces lighter or darker).

THE TV PICTURE

Field of view
The camera sees only a 4-by-3 rectangular wedge from the entire scene. The audience is unaware of whatever lies outside that segment

The camera is selective
When shots show the entire scene, or the person standing, the wall shading is effective. But in the seated shot, it is not visible

13

What does *Lighting* involve?

You can apply lighting know-how to any situation you are shooting. Even when the light that is already there, happens to give excellent results, a knowledge of lighting principles can help you towards more effective picture-making. Simply by angling the subject or repositioning it, or altering the camera's viewpoint, you will often find that you can considerably improve picture impact. Sometimes, you can enhance the existing lighting by reflecting light onto the subject from another angle, or adding some extra illumination.

Daylight, as you will see, is extremely variable. The illumination within buildings can take many forms; from fluorescent-bank ceilings to localized pools of light. It is important to bear in mind that even though local lighting may be very appropriate for normal activities there, that does not mean that it will suit the video camera. Ugly effects that we overlook on the spot thanks to our ability to adapt to local conditions can appear quite grotesque on the screen, e.g. the deep black eye sockets produced by overhead lighting.

The amount of lighting needed

If there is already sufficient light around, will it be appropriate for your purpose? Is its direction, strength, contrast, color quality satisfactory? If for some reason the existing lighting is unsatisfactory, you may need to provide the entire illumination for the scene.

There is no regular set-up that will automatically ensure successful lighting. Sometimes, all you need to produce the optimum pictorial effect, is a single carefully angled lamp. For many purposes, three lamps may be a minimum. But there are situations where a dozen or more lighting fixtures are essential if you want to build up a particular effect.

The complexity of lighting needed, will depend on a number of factors, such as:

The area appearing in the shot(s) – It is a lot easier to cope with a close shot, than a large expanse such as an open arena, a large hall.

The nature of the action – Whether the subject is stationary or moving around.

The nature of the subject – Some subjects are much more critical to light than others.

The artistic effect – Treatment that is great when demonstrating machinery, will be quite inappropriate for an interview.

Unsuitable available light
Although there may be light on the
scene, it may not be appropriate for
your shots, or it may create
unattractive effects

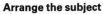

Arrange the subject
Sometimes you can position the
subject to suit the available lighting

Augment the light
You may be able to use the available
light, and augment it to improve the
results

Special lighting
There will be situations where you
can only achieve the best results by
using a series of specially positioned
lamps

The aims of lighting

Your main preoccupations when lighting any situation are usually with:

The appearance of the *subject* itself; and
The appearance of its *surroundings.*

If you are shooting a fairly restricted area, the same set of lighting may suit both. But for larger areas or more complex situations, it is generally necessary to light subjects and backgrounds separately.

Lighting the subject

According to the way you arrange light, you can *emphasize* certain characteristic features of the subject, make them *less obvious*, or *conceal* them altogether. Your approach will depend on which aspects are most appropriate for the occasion. Through selective lighting treatment you can, for instance, draw attention to the irregularities of a worn surface, or suggest how delicate and fragile a subject is.

In most cases, *clarity* is important. You will want your picture to have a three-dimensional quality; building up an impression of solidity and depth. But conversely, you can equally well arrange light to create the illusion of a flat two-dimensional image.

Casual lighting treatment produces unpredictable or haphazard results. You may find for instance, that shading or shadows obscure important detail, or that texture and form are lost in the picture.

Incorrect lighting can spoil the shot

If the lighting treatment is wrong for a particular shot, various problems can arise. Distracting picture blemishes, such as *lens flares* can develop. Strong specular burned-out highlights reflecting from shiny surfaces may distract the eye.

A person's shadow falling onto a map, may prevent our reading information there. Someone may be describing delicate carving. . . which is virtually invisible on camera, due to flat lighting. We may be unable to see details of an oil painting, due to light glare on its surface. People may appear unattractive, haggard, ageing – even ill – if inappropriately lit.

Decorative lighting

You can use light to create a wide range of decorative effects. These add visual appeal, engender a mood, charm the eye, and encourage interest. You must ensure that the picture not only conveys its message, but is enjoyable to watch.

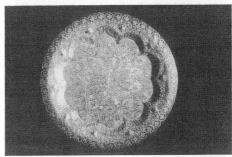

Visibility
It is not enough to just illuminate the subject, so that it is visible

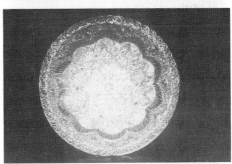

Clarity
When effectively lit, all the detail in this dish is clearly visible. But use an inappropriate lighting angle, and much of it disappears!

Effectiveness
Poorly arranged lighting can actually prevent the audience from seeing the subject being demonstrated!

17

The character of light

There are certain aspects of light that particularly interest us here, for they directly affect what the subject looks like on the screen:

1. The light's *quality or dispersion*.
   Light quality can range:
   - From the very directional *hard light* that casts distinct, well-defined shadows (e.g., from sunlight, spotlights).
   - To the diffuse, shadowless *soft light* that is scattered from broad light sources or a sunless sky.
2. The light's *direction* relative to your camera's viewpoint. This will have a considerable influence on the appearance of the subject and the scene. Reposition the camera, and the effective lighting direction changes.
3. The *color quality or color temperature* of the light. What we regard as *'white light'* is often, in fact, noticeably reddish, yellowish, or bluish, as the camera reveals. So unless the system is reasonably matched to the color temperature of the lighting, the picture can have a pronounced color cast.

The influence of light

Because eye and brain adjust so readily to prevailing light conditions, we usually accept even wide variations without a second thought. We subconsciously interpret, we make assumptions, and at times even 'see' effects that are not actually there!

You will often find that there are considerable differences between your on-the-spot assessments, and the way the impartial camera interprets the scene. When shooting outdoors on a dull overcast day for instance, pictures can be disappointingly flat and uninteresting, although the scene itself looks attractive enough to the eye. As the sun moves round the sky, shadow formations and subject modeling alter noticeably. We tend to overlook these changes, but they are very obvious when we compare shots taken at different times.

Part of the 'magic' of effective lighting treatment, lies in the ways you can control the appearance of subject and scene, by carefully blending the light quality and selecting the light direction.

Light quality
Hard light casts clear-cut shadows, and reveals the modeling and texture of surfaces

Soft light is diffused and shadowless. It illuminates subjects without emphasizing their surface contours or texture

The influence of light
You can alter the appearance of a subject, by the kind of light you use to illuminate it, and the direction of the light: soft overall, hard steep frontal, side light, double-rim back light

19

The color quality of light

It is easy to overlook the *color quality* of the light when you are shooting. But if you do so, you may have some surprises in store when viewing the final pictures! Some will appear 'warm' (orange tint), others 'cold' (blue tint). People shot on location in mixed lighting may have an orange and blue complexion! So let's look more closely at this phenomenon.

The light spectrum
Project a beam of 'white' light through a prism, and you will see that it disperses into a progressive range of colors — covering a *visible spectrum* from red, orange, yellow, green, blue, indigo, through to violet. If you analyze the color quality of any kind of 'white' light source, you will find that the actual *proportions* of these component colors vary considerably.

To compare and classify these variations in 'white' light sources, a system of measurement known as the *Kelvin scale* is used, in which the source's overall color temperature is measured in *Kelvin units* (K).

Varying color temperature
Generally speaking, *daylight* includes a high proportion of blue light — it has a *high color temperature*. But its actual color quality varies considerably with weather conditions and the time of day.

Light from *tungsten lamps* is comparatively lacking at the blue end of the spectrum; i.e., it has a *lower color temperature*, and appears much more yellow–orange in character. As tungsten lamps (regular or T-H types) are dimmed, the color temperature of their light falls, becoming noticeably orange–yellow; a fact you need to bear in mind when dimming lamps to reduce their intensity.

Matching
Video and photographic systems are color-balanced to produce optimum color accuracy when used with white light of a particular chromatic quality — e.g., for use in daylight (5500 K), or tungsten light (3200 or 3400 K). Ideally, your lighting and the system's color standard should match, but you will usually find that variations in color temperature of ±150 K (e.g., 3100–2800 K) are acceptable.

However, if you use tungsten lighting with a system balanced for daylight, the color picture will have an appreciable orange–yellow cast. Conversely, shooting in daylight with a tungsten-balanced system, results in strong blue tint.

COLOR TEMPERATURE

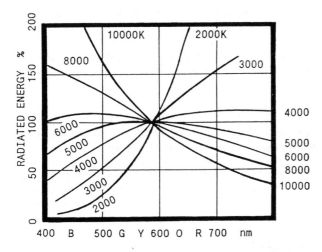

As the color temperature varies, the relative proportions of each part of the spectrum change. (Here the curves are centered about an arbitrary 580 μm, to make comparisons simpler)

Typical color temperatures (in Kelvins)

Standard candle	1930
Household tungsten lamps * 25–250 w	2600–2900
Studio tungsten lamps * 500–1000 w	3000
Studio tungsten lamps * 2000 w	3275
Studio tungsten lamps * 5 kw, 10 kw	3380
Tungsten-halogen lamps ('quartz lights')	3200–3400
Overrun tungsten lamps (Photoflood) *	3400–3500
Fluorescent lamps	3200–7500
High intensity arcs	4000–6200
HMI arcs	5600–6000
Xenon arc or flash	6000

Daylight

Sunrise, sunset	2000–3000
Sunless early morn, late afternoon	4500–4800
Midday sun	5000–5400
Summer sun plus blue sky light	5500–6500
Overcast sky	6800–7500
Summer shade	6000–7000
Hazy sky	8000
Clear blue north sky	10,000–20,000

* Run at their correct, full voltage. Lamps using a supply voltage below 240 volts operate at higher temperatures (e.g. 50–100 K).

Correcting color temperature

When video camera circuits are adjusted, they are usually *set up* (*lined up*) to suit a 'standard' color balance, which will reasonably match the color temperature of tungsten lighting (e.g., 3200 K and 2950 K).

But what if you are shooting in lighting of an appreciably higher or lower color temperature than your camera's setting? You have several options:

1. *Accept* the color discrepancies. For artistic reasons, you may actually want the picture to have a warmer or cooler color quality than normal.
2. If you are shooting in *daylight with a video camera* balanced to *tungsten (3200 K)*, you can:

   - Switch the camera's color-balance circuits from 'tungsten' to 'daylight' (5600 K), using either preset or manual controls.
   - Press the camera's *'white balance'* button while shooting a white surface, to automatically rebalance its circuits.
   - Shoot through an orange–brown compensatory color filter (e.g., Wratten 85) – either selected on a filter wheel within the camera, or clipped over its lens.
   - Place Wratten 85 acrylic sheets or plastic film over windows. These can be combined with neutral density filters if necessary, to reduce the daylight intensity at the same time.

If you are shooting in *daylight with a camera* that is color balanced to *daylight*, there are no problems. But use it in *total tungsten light*, and you will need to rebalance the camera (to 3200 K), alter its filter (to Wratten 81 blue), or put blue filter medium over the tungsten lighting fixtures.

When you use auxiliary tungsten lighting while shooting in daylight, either the daylit areas will look too blue, or the tungsten lit areas appear too orange. Again, filtering is the answer. If your camera is balanced to daylight, you will need blue filters or dichroics over your lamps (with a slight light loss). Alternatively, with the camera balanced to tungsten, you will need to place orange filters over windows.

Mireds

The effect of any color correction/conversion filter is greatest with high color temperature sources. *Mired units* help you to calculate the filter required to convert one color temperature to another. The table opposite shows that if you want to raise a 4000 K light source (250 mireds) to about 5000 K (200 mireds) a 50 mired filter is needed (i.e., 250–200). Place the same *filter* over a 300 K source, and this will provide a 500 K shift to 3500 K.

COLOR BALANCE –
WHITE BALANCE

MATCHED BALANCE
The video camera
should be adjusted to
suit the color quality of
the light; e.g. daylight,
tungsten lighting

Mixed luminants
If the illumination is a
mixture of tungsten
and daylight, one or the
other will produce very
inaccurate color values.
You can't match the
camera to *both*

**Compensatory light
filters**
When lighting is mixed,
put a color filter over
one source (e.g. a blue
filter on the tungsten
lamps), and color
balance the camera to
the other (e.g. daylight)

Kelvin to mired shift

Kelvins	0	100	200	300	400	500	600	700	800	900
2000	500	476	455	435	417	400	385	370	357	345
3000	333	323	312	303	294	286	278	270	263	256
4000	250	244	238	233	227	222	217	213	208	204
5000	200	196	192	189	185	182	179	175	172	169
6000	167	164	161	159	156	154	152	149	147	145
7000	143	140	139	137	135	133	132	130	128	126
8000	125	123	122	120	119	118	116	115	114	112
9000	111	110	109	108	106	105	104	103	102	101

Example: The conversion number for 4500 K is 222 mireds.

Mired to kelvin shift

Mireds	0	10	20	30	40	50	60	70	80	90
100	10,000	9090	8333	7692	7143	6667	6250	5882	5556	5263
200	5000	4762	4546	4347	4167	4000	3846	3703	3571	3448
300	3333	3226	3125	3030	2941	2857	2778	2703	2631	2564

Example: A filter of e.g. 250 mireds converts to 4000 K.

$$\text{Mireds} = \frac{1,000,000}{\text{Kelvin}} \qquad \text{Decamireds} \frac{100,000}{\text{Kelvins}} = \frac{\text{mireds}}{10}$$

23

Typical light sources

Various luminants are used in video/TV lighting. Each has its particular advantages and limitations relative to cost, efficiency, light output, life, size and color quality.

Tungsten lamps/incandescent bulbs
Tungsten lamps have the disadvantages that their light output and color temperature (3200 K; 312 mireds) fall considerably in use. Those used for video/television lighting range from 150–10 000 watts. The domestic tungsten bulbs fitted in 'practical' decorative lamps are typically 15–150 watts.

Tungsten-halogen bulbs (T-H)/quartz lights
These improved tungsten lamps have a halogen gas filling which increases their efficiency, giving a nearly constant output and color quality throughout a longer life. They are available in compact point-source and linear (tubular) forms, to suit all types of lighting fixtures. Avoid handling quartz bulbs (it discolors and damages their surface). Versions using 'hard glass' are cheaper, but shorter-lived.

Overrun lamps
These tungsten or quartz lights are designed to give a greater output than normal for their wattage. The price for increased light, and a higher color temperature (3400 K) is a shortened life (e.g., 2–100 hours). Useful for lightweight portable fittings, but liable to break down unexpectedly.

PAR/sealed-beam/internal-reflector lamps
Regular and overrun versions are made in tungsten (incandescent) and tungsten-halogen forms. The bulb's front may be clear, frosted, or molded into a lens. The inner surface of its shaped bulb is silvered to provide an in-built reflector, which pre-focuses the light beam. Lightweight and very adaptable, with wide or narrow coverage, these lamps need only a basic protective housing (no additional lens or reflector).

Metal halide lamps
In HMI, CSI and CID forms, these very efficient enclosed arc lamps have a considerable light output at a high color temperature (5500 K) matching well with daylight. However, a bulky starter/ballast unit is necessary to regulate the arc's current.

Other sources
Fluorescent lamps can provide diffuse illumination, but their uneven color quality and low output limit their value. *Carbon arcs* have restricted burning time, and need continual attention, so are little used in video production.

Tungsten lamps
Relatively cheap, but their output and color quality deteriorate badly in use.
A Low wattage lamps (domestic)
B Bipost base (fresnel spotlight)
C GES base (Scoop)

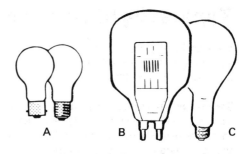

Tungsten-halogen lamps/quartz lights
Compact adaptable light sources of constant output and color temperature. Extremely hot and brittle in use.
A Fresnel spotlight
B Lensless spot
C Cyc light
D Scoop
E Effects projectors/ellipsoidal spots

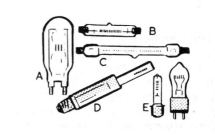

Internal-reflector lamps (A)
PAR lamps (B)
The lamp's inner surface forms a reflector, which directs and focuses the light. Available in flood and spot versions. No adjustments possible, but clip-on accessories control the light beam.

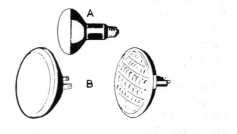

Metal-halide lamps
High efficiency, high output sources with high color temperature. But requiring ignitor/ballast units. Take time to reach full intensity. Switch-on is delayed when hot. Needs a.c. supply
(A) CSI   (B) HMI

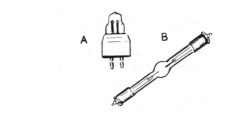

Fluorescent lighting
Economical but bulky. Limited output. Dubious color quality. Large area illumination only. Not easily localized

25

Hard light

'Hard light' gives a picture definition and vigor, and is essential to create a three-dimensional illusion.

The features of hard light
Most of the lighting fixtures you use are likely to be hard light sources, for the sharp well-defined shadows they cast help you to reveal shape, contours and texture in subject and scene. Hard light is invaluable, too, when building up an environmental illusion through the cast shadows of windows, trees, etc. Decorative light-patterns of many kinds create attractive scenic effects.

Hard light has the great advantage that it is easily controlled. You can shape, restrict or reflect the light beam as you wish.

The limitations of hard light
Hard light has to be used carefully. Strong modeling and dramatic shadows give a picture a dynamic appeal but, badly or inapppropriately used, hard light can produce crude modeling and coarse tonal contrasts. Shadows can be unattractive or distracting, and obscure important details in the subject.

Hard light sources
Two forms of hard light source are widely used in video production. The lightweight *lensless spotlight* ('redhead', *external reflector spot*), relies on a concave reflector to concentrate the light from its small quartz (T-H) lamp. The *'fresnel spotlight'* has an additional, stepped *fresnel lens* system to focus the light beam. This arrangement is used in many forms of spotlight, from hand-held units to large carbon arcs. The light beam may have a hard or softened edge; the latter being more easily blended into nearby lit areas.

Moving the lamp and its reflector, adjusts the beam width from *fully spotted* to a *fully flooded* coverage (often with some change in light intensity and evenness).

Projection spotlights (profile spots, ellipsoidal spots)
These fixtures are designed to project precisely-shaped light beams (using internal shutters), shadows/light-patterns from metal stencils (*gobos*), or glass slides. The size of the projected image depends on the fixture's distance from the background, and its lens system. Some versions can also project moving pattern effects.

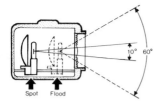

HARD LIGHT

Fresnel spotlight
The fresnel lens produces a very even light beam, with a softened edge that allows adjacent lamps to be overlapped unobtrusively for continuous overall illumination. Beam coverage and intensity alter as the lamp/reflector are moved

Projection spotlight/ellipsoidal spotlight/profile spot
The shape of the hard-edged light beam can be adjusted (internal blades). Patterns of adjustable hardness can be projected, using metal stencils (*gobos*)

Revealing shadows
Under hard light, shadows can reveal information that was not visible under soft illumination

Shadow patterns
Shadows are decorative or distracting. While the window pattern is effective in a long shot, it can produce unattractive effects in the close shot

27

The lensless spotlight

Known variously as a *lensless spotlight, external reflector spot, open-bulb spot, open-faced fixture, 'Redhead', 'Blonde*, this form of spotlight is widely used on location, and in studios.

Basic design
The unit is basically an open-fronted reinforced plastic shell. Inside is a small bare quartz-light (tungsten halogen lamp) located within a compact adjustable reflector. Because there is no lens system, the unit is much lighter than a fresnel spotlight (1.5–4 kg/3.3–8.8 lb). As there are no lens light-losses, it has a high overall efficiency. You can adjust the beam-spread and the light intensity by moving the lamp's position with a screw knob or a sweep lever (slider) at the rear of the unit.

The lensless spotlight can be fitted with various accessories, including dichroic daylight filters, stainless steel mesh 'scrims' and barndoors.

Supporting the fixture
You can support the lensless spot in several ways:

• Fixed into a lightweight lighting stand.
• Clamped to an overhead or vertical spring-pole.
• Attached to the setting, walls, doors, furniture etc., with a heavy grip (gaffer grip/gator clip).
• Mounted on a wall plate (nailed, screwed or taped to walls).
• Hand held.

Advantages
This type of fixture is lightweight, very efficient, and extremely versatile. The output from a *800 W* lensless spotlight (spotted) is only half a stop down on a 2 kW fresnel tungsten spot covering the same area. Because it has a +80° coverage (compared with typical fresnel 60°) it can cover a wide area, even in confined spaces.

Disadvantages
The light beam is somewhat uneven, varying with focusing (central hotspot or darker patch). Some designs have noticeable light fall-off at the beam edge. Barndoor flaps only provide a gradual light cut-off; insufficient for some purposes.

Applications
Particularly valuable when power and ventilation are limited, the spotlight can be used as a *key, back light* or to light backgrounds. You can even use it as a soft source by bouncing light from the ceiling or a reflector board, or using heavy diffusion – diffuser clipped on the extended barndoor flaps.

THE LENSLESS SPOTLIGHT

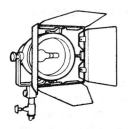

Power
Smaller versions typically: 800 W
220/240 V, or 600/650 W 120 V, or
250 W 30 V 80 mm linear quartz
lamps (3200–3400 K). Larger
versions: 1000 W or 2000 W 120 V
lamps

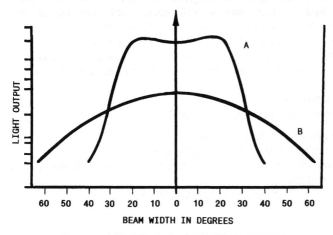

BEAM WIDTH IN DEGREES

A.   2kW FRESNEL SPOTLIGHT (FULLY FLOODED)

B.   LENSLESS SPOT (FULLY SPOTTED)

Compared coverage
Here the gradual light fall-off across the beam of a typical lensless spotlight,
is compared with the very even coverage of a 2 kW fresnel spot

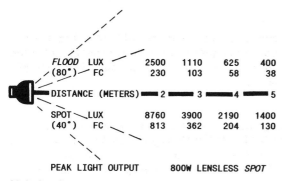

FLOOD LUX	2500	1110	625	400
(80°) FC	230	103	58	38
DISTANCE (METERS)	2	3	4	5
SPOT LUX	8760	3900	2190	1400
(40°) FC	813	362	204	130

PEAK LIGHT OUTPUT   800W LENSLESS *SPOT*

Light level
Showing how the light level of a typical external reflector spotlight falls with
distance. (Center of beam)

Soft light

Most effective lighting is a subtle blend of hard and soft light. Although the main light sources are generally *spotlights*, you will usually want to control their shadows and the tonal contrast, by introducing a certain amount of soft *fill light*.

When used as a 'soft key', diffused light provides delicately graduated shading and half-tones. But it should be angled to the camera's lens-axis to avoid reducing surface modeling and texture.

For 'high-key' or 'day-exterior' scenes in the studio, you can flood an area with a soft overall *base light* to keep tonal contrast to a minimum, without creating further shadows. But excessive soft light washes out surface modeling, and produces flat uninteresting pictures.

Soft light has disadvantages

Unlike focused hard light, a soft light's effective strength falls off rapidly with distance. So it may overlight a nearby subject, yet be insufficiently bright for a more distant one. (A particular problem with 'soft keys'.) Soft light is not readily restricted. It is liable to spill around and overlight backgrounds. Even quite large light-shields (gobos) will not localize the light if it is truly diffuse.

Soft light sources

Ideally, 'soft light' units should produce diffuse, absolutely shadowless illumination. In practice though, design is a compromise, for the lighting fixtures need to be reasonably compact.

The simplest 'soft light' fixtures have a single open bulb within a reflector; in the form of an open dish (*scoop*) or a trough (*broad*). The light is not particularly soft; faint shadows are usually discernible. Units can be suspended singly or grouped, fitted to lighting stands or rested on the floor. A series of troughs can be suspended and/or rest on the floor, to illuminate backgrounds (*cyc lights*, *grounds rows*, *strip lights*).

In '*softlite/softlight*' sources, the light from hidden internal lamps is scattered within the unit to produce diffuse illumination.

Multi-lamp designs rely on the overlapping light from a series of bulbs to produce soft light. In *floodlight banks* a group of three to twelve 650 watt *PAR* bulbs with switched and adjustable sections, provides a powerful soft light source.

The illumination from all soft light units can be diffused further with clip-on frosted plastic medium, or spun-glass sheets.

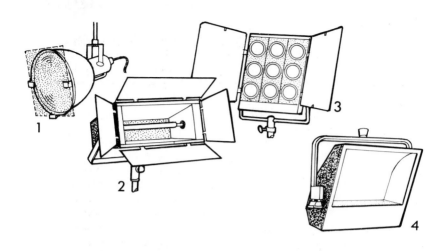

USING SOFT LIGHT

Soft light fixtures

These widely used forms of soft light fixtures include

1 a large open reflector (*scoop*), 2 small reflector with line filament (*broad*), 3 multiple lamp source (*floodlight bank*), and 4 internally reflected designs (*large broad, 'softlite'*)

Using fill light

1 Lit with a hard key alone, shadow areas may be too dense; information may be lost
2 An appropriate amount of fill light reveals information, without destroying form and modeling
3 Under excess fill light, the modeling created by the key light is lost

How much light is needed?

Obviously more sensitive camera systems need less light. And in darker surroundings, more illumination may be necessary than in a light-toned environment for more light is absorbed by subjects, and less reflected towards the camera. In practice, the average amount of light your video camera needs to produce high quality pictures is largely determined by the *lens aperture (f/*stop).

Smaller apertures reduce the lens image intensity, and so require more light on the scene. But they provide a greater *depth of field*; i.e., more of the scene is in sharp focus. Larger apertures increase the lens image intensity so less light is needed. However, at the same time focused depth is correspondingly reduced, and sharp focusing is more difficult.

In the studio one tends to work to a 'standard' light level (e.g., 800 lux/75 foot candles at around *f/*4.5). This *f/*stop provides sufficient depth of field, yet does not require the high light levels that cause dazzle, ventilation problems, high power costs, larger lighting fixtures, etc. As reducing the lens aperture from *f/*4 to *f/*5.6 requires double the original light level on the scene, clearly lens apertures are not chosen casually!

On location, lens apertures are usually chosen to suit the prevailing lighting conditions, and any additional illumination you introduce must be balanced to this setting.

Exposure

The camera's image sensor (pickup device) needs a certain amount of light from all parts of the scene, to produce an image with a wide tonal range. If there is too little light around, the picture will be *under exposed*) and shadow details lost. (Underexposure may also cause distracting visual defects.)

You may compensate by opening up the *lens aperture* (larger *f/*stop; smaller number), but this will limit the *depth of field*. (Increasing the camera's *video gain* makes the overall picture brighter, but does not overcome any picture defects.)

Too much light for a given lens aperture produces an *over-exposed* shot. All tones reproduce unnaturally light, and the lightest are crushed out. Reducing the lens aperture (*stopping down*) corrects the exposure and correspondingly increases the focused depth.

Relative light intensities

Sometimes a subject appears insufficiently lit, because the lens has been stopped down to compensate for an overlit background. Rather than increase the subject's lighting further, it may be better to reduce background lighting, and open up the lens a little.

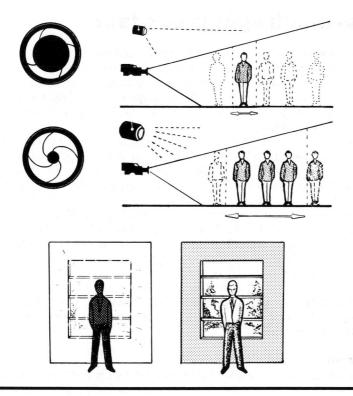

THE AMOUNT OF LIGHT NEEDED

Lens aperture (*f*-stop)
When light levels are lower, the lens aperture must be opened up (e.g. to *f*/2) for correct exposure, and the depth of field will be limited. At high light levels the lens will be stopped down (e.g. to *f*/16) for correct exposure, and the depth of field increases considerably

Relative exposures
If you stop the lens down, the extra light now needed to maintain exposure is:

$$\frac{(second\ f\ number)^2}{(first\ f\ number)^2}$$

Supposing you stop down from *f*/4 to *f*/8:

$$\frac{8^2}{4^2} = \frac{64}{16} = \frac{4}{1}$$

So light levels need to be increased fourfold to maintain the same exposure

Relative brightness
Against an overbright background, the subject appears insufficiently lit. Open the lens aperture to expose the subject correctly, and reduce the background brightness

Is much equipment needed?

There is no simple rule, for a lot depends on the complexity and size of the production, and how elaborate your treatment is to be. You may be limited by facilities, time or space.

Production treatment
The nature of the action, and the way it is going to be shot, will influence how much equipment you need. If two people sit close together they can share the lighting. Put further apart, they will have to be lit separately. The more positions and directions the performers have, the more complex the lighting is likely to be – unless you are content with general overall treatment. Shots taking in a lot of background are likely to need more extensive lighting than closer shots. Lighting often grows more elaborate as camera viewpoints increase. Any lighting changes may increase the number of lamps needed; particularly where there are color variations. Light patterns and special lighting effects require separate careful treatment.

Simplicity or elaboration?
A single lamp can produce an impressive dramatic effect. Yet it may take dozens to create a scene that looks completely natural!

You can economize by having one lamp do several jobs (e.g., as a key, back light, background lighting). But does it do all these things well? Or are the angle and intensity a poor compromise? A treatment that is too basic can result in bland uninteresting pictures that miss visual opportunities.

Over-elaborate treatments on the other hand, can look fussy and fragmented. Complex lighting is also liable to cause multiple shadows and conflicting light directions, with one lamp spoiling the effects produced by another.

Practical considerations
Sometimes it pays to *simplify*. You cannot rely on inexperienced talent to stand at marked floor positions. They are quite likely to move out of the key, into the bright beam of a lamp modeling dark drapes nearby! In these circumstances, it may be safer to apply a broader treatment, rather than localized lighting.

If you simplify by covering a large area with a single lamp, you may find it too steep when the performer is close. You might find that two separate lamps would be more controllable.

Sometimes *elaboration* has its advantages. Arrange several different key angles for a violinist at a concert, and you can select which proves to be most suitable as he/she turns around while playing.

Basic lighting
If the lighting treatment is too
basic, the result will be crude and
unattractive

Elaborate lighting
Elaborate treatment may give
greater flexibility, or lead to a
confused, disjointed effect,
depending on how skillfully it is
applied

Balanced lighting
A well-balanced lighting treatment
is both adaptable, and direct;
without over-decoration or
unnecessary emphasis

35

How are lamps supported?

The smallest lighting fixtures can be hand-held or camera-mounted and are particularly useful when working in confined spaces. The *camera-light* (*basher*, *headlamp*) can serve as a key light, frontal fill-light, or to supplement other illumination.

Hung lamps

Smaller studios are usually fitted with a lighting *pipe-grid* just below a typically 3.5 m/12 ft high ceiling. Lamps are clamped, clipped or slung from this tubular lattice structure. Power outlets for these fixtures are provided in the ceiling or along the grid.

Larger studios have systems including independently suspended motorized battens (bars), or a slotted ceiling grid into which telescopic lamp-hangers fit. Some studios also have catwalks (walkways) high around the walls, where manned lamps (e.g., follow spotlights) can be arranged.

Stand lamps

Lighting stands (*floor stands*) allow you to position lamps quickly and accurately, anywhere between, e.g., 0.3–2.5 m/1 ft–8 ft from floor level. However, although more easily adjusted than hung lamps, stand lamps have the disadvantages that they can be accidentally displaced or over-balanced. And their trailing cables need to be secured out of the way of cameras and passing feet. Because lighting stands can obstruct very mobile cameras (and cast camera shadows!), they are mainly used at the edges of settings, or offstage, e.g. to provide 'sunlight' through windows.

Additional supports

Particularly on location, where one needs to improvize, you can arrange lamps on telescopic *support* poles wedged between floor and ceiling or wall-to-wall, within corridors, arches, window openings, doorways, etc.

An endless range of devices enables you to clamp lightweight lighting fixtures to nearby walls, furniture, pipes, etc. Various adjustable clamps (clip lights, 'gator-grips'), brackets, screw plates, suction cups, even *gaffer tape* (adhesive plasticized cloth tape), readily attach lamps to any surface.

Hidden lamps

When lighting otherwise inaccessible backgrounds, ceilings, etc., it is sometimes necessary to hide fixtures behind scenery or furniture (on stands, or on the ground).

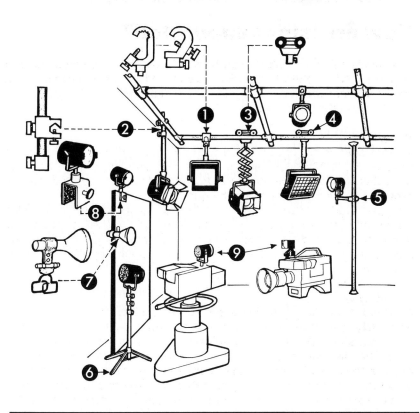

LAMP SUPPORTS

In smaller studios, a ceiling *pipe-grid* supports suspended equipment – on
1.25 in diameter (31.75 mm) tube at 4–8 ft (1.2–2.4 m) intervals

1 Clamped directly to the grid (*C-clamp* fitting)
2 Lowered from an extendable concentric tube (*hanger*; drop arm)
3 Movable trolley with *pantograph* (extends 0.05–3.6 m/2–12 ft)
4 Telescopic hanger (*telescope, monopole, skyhook*)
5 In confined space, spring-loaded support pole (*polecat, barracuda*);
  wedged between walls, or floor and ceiling
6 Telescopic *lighting stand* (0.45–2.7 m/1.5–9 ft)
7 *Clip lamp* (*spring clamp*) attached to a scenic flat
8 *Scenic bracket*; screws to edge or top of flat
9 *Camera light* (*headlamp, basher*)

The effect of light direction

An object's appearance can change considerably with the angle of the light. Fortunately, any effect of light direction is really a variation on three extremes – *frontal*, *edge* (*side*) and *back* light. You can study these basic light directions for yourself with a flashlight in a darkened room.

Frontal lighting

In any picture we judge a subject's shape by the way shadows are cast across its surface and background, and noting how light shades off round surface contours. The tiny shadows produced by small surface irregularities we recognize as 'texture'.

If you shine light directly onto a subject from around the lens position (*dead frontal*) it will cast *no* shadows that are visible in the shot. So you cannot see surface contours or texture clearly. The lighting is *flat*.

As you move the frontal light, some 10°–50° from the lens position, shadows and shading grow in the opposite direction, and any unevenness on the surface becomes increasingly obvious.

One side of the subject appears brighter than the other, and planes furthest from the lamp begin to darken. With a face, the nose shadow spreads across a cheek.

Edge light (side light)

At sunset and dawn, the sun's light casts long shadows, and exaggerates land contours as it skims over it at a shallow angle. Similarly, you can emphasize texture and shape, using light that is almost in line with a surface. Even slight irregularities in wood, stone, paper, fabric, become clearly visible under *edge lighting*. The smallest details are revealed in a close-up coin, or carved bas-relief.

When the light is directly above a subject, it is usually called *top light*; while from either side, it becomes *side light*. But both are actually forms of edge light – although they will emphasize different aspects of the subject.

Back light

As you move a lamp round behind a subject, the front of it falls into shadow from your viewpoint. (The far side of it is now well lit of course, as another camera position could reveal.) All you will now see of the subject will be some light around its edges – in the case of a person, on the top of the head and shoulders. However, if the subject is translucent, it will now appear strongly lit, and the *back light* will effectively reveal its structure and form.

LIGHTING DIRECTION

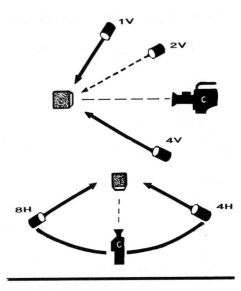

Frontal lighting
The main frontal lamp or *key light*, is normally the main light source, and largely determines exposure

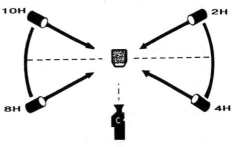

Side light
Side light emphasizes contour and texture, throwing them into strong relief; but can create an unbalanced lop-sided effect

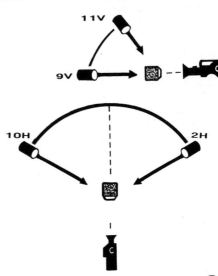

Back light
Back light rims the edges and tops of subjects; shining through translucent or transparent planes

39

Where do you place the lamps?

You have now met the principles that underly all lighting techniques: the characteristics of *hard light* and *soft light*, and the three main *light directions*. These are the basics from which all lighting treatment is developed!

Three-point lighting

The simplest complete lighting set-up is an arrangement often called *three-point lighting*. Fundamentally this approach consists of the main *key light*, a *fill light* or *filler*, and a *back light*. You do not always need all three lamps. Occasionally a single key light alone will suffice. Sometimes an extra lamp or two may be needed. But this is an effective working approach.

The *key light* is the strongest lamp: the main source of illumination. Technically, it usually determines the exposure. Artistically, it establishes the light direction, and creates the principal modeling and shadow formations. Its most effective angle will depend on the subject you are lighting; its position, and which aspects you want to emphasize. The environment (e.g., a nearby window) will also influence the angle you choose. If you use *two* or *more* key lights on the same subject, they will probably conflict; confusing modeling, and creating distracting multiple shadow formations.

The *fill light* (*filler, fill-in*) illuminates the shadow areas produced by the key light. Not too strongly, for you do not want to swamp the effect created by the key. Remember, the fill light always has a supplementary role. It should never dominate. You may sometimes light successfully without using any fill light at all; especially if the key is quite frontal. But results may prove rather more contrasty and dramatic than is appropriate.

Some people use *back light* as a routine, but to be really effective, you should choose its direction and intensity carefully. Back light illuminates the edge-contours of the subject. It often reveals their depth and form. Particularly where the subject and background tones are similar, back light will help to create a more three-dimensional illusion. Without it, planes within the picture are liable to merge, so that the overall result is flat and lacking vitality.

Designating direction

To indicate a lamp's position in space quickly you need a simple, easily remembered, unambiguous system. In practice, many people find it a lot easier to judge positions accurately, using 'clock face' references (as in the scheme opposite) than to estimate actual angular differences (5 minutes = 30°).

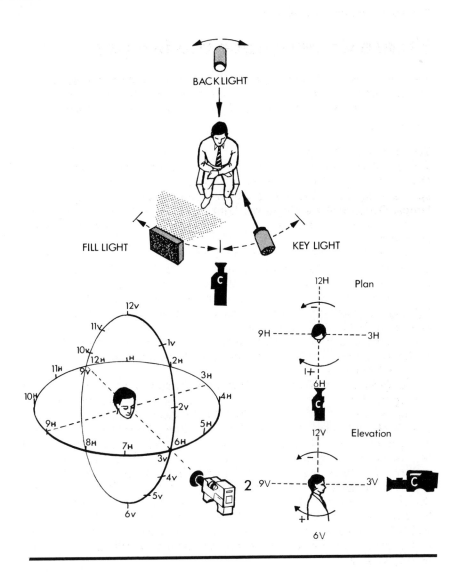

PLACING THE LAMPS

Three-point lighting
This basic three-light set-up can be used for lighting most three-dimensional subjects

Specifying light positions
To describe the position of a lamp in space, it is often easiest to think of the subject as being in the center of a horizontal clock face (for direction), and a vertical clock face (for height). The camera is at position **6H/3V**. ('Hours' represent 30° steps; 'minutes' are 6° each)

Positioning the key light

Whether the position of the key light is critical or not really depends on the subject itself, the effect you are aiming at, and your standards. Some people will find a particular shadow ugly (e.g., a long nose shadow, or a shadow on the wall behind a subject), others will overlook it.

Your main aim is usually to create an attractive effect, with an appropriate amount of modeling. Not too little, so that the subject looks flat or featureless; nor too much or the modeling may be coarsely crude and unattractive.

For many subjects, the key light's angle can be anywhere between 10° to 50° off the lens' central axis. For people, wide-angled keys are generally less successful.

Sometimes your will find that the position you would prefer for your key light causes problems – ugly shadows, spurious reflections, distracting hot-spots, sound boom shadows. Then you may need to compromise to some extent, and reposition the key for practical rather than artistic reasons.

Choosing the best position

It is easy to simply place the key somewhere in front of the subject beside the camera as a mechanical routine. But 'making the subject visible' is not enough. Remember, the key's angle affects *what the subject looks like*.

Starting with the key beside the lens move it to one side. You will see that shadows move *in the opposite direction*. The more you angle the light, the more these shadows will grow or be displaced. Raise the lamp, and shadows move downwards. These simple principles are an important guide to the key position; the angle at which you want shadows to form on the subject.

Suppose you are lighting a person who is wearing a cap. As you steepen the key's angle, its peak shadow moves down, covering the wearer's eyes. Now you have to make a decision. Do you want the eyes hidden in shadow this way – for dramatic effect? Do you add fill light to illuminate the shadow? Or finding the shadow intrusive, do you lower the key to shorten it? (Perhaps you tilt the head or the cap back – or remove it!)

The key does not have to be *frontal*. Sometimes the most interesting features of the subject are not facing the camera (as in a profile). Then it may be better to position the key to one side, rather than frontal.

Where a subject is translucent, transparent, or has outline tracery, it may be most effective to key it from *behind*; depending on which aspects you most want to display, or to emphasize.

PLACING THE KEY LIGHT

Non-critical key light direction
Some subjects can be presented effectively, using a wide range of lighting treatments. This item looks interesting, when lit with a side key (with and without fill light), or treated as a silhouette

Critical key direction
With other subjects the key light's direction needs to be chosen carefully, or the audience will be unable to see important features

Positioning the fill light

Fill light or filler (*fill-in*) is too often used casually, overdone, or even ignored. In video/TV studios, soft light is often hung, rather than supported on lighting stands. Although this leaves the floor clear for cameras to move around more freely, it does mean that the fill light will tend to be much steeper; especially when close to the subject.

The character of fill light

Ideally, fill light should always be diffused (soft). It should illuminate shadows sufficiently to reveal detail, without spoiling the modeling created by the key light. Excess fill light flattens modeling. If there is insufficient, modeling is liable to be too harsh – unless, of course, you particularly want a dramatic impact.

Soft light falls off rapidly with distance, and tends to spill around, illuminating the surroundings. This can be a problem where, for instance, you need *localized* fill light for an isolated subject; e.g., a spotlight singer on a darkened stage. In this particular situation it may be better to use a low-intensity diffused spotlight to provide fill light instead, and rely on the strong key light to dilute any subsidiary shadows.

Fill light sources

For a fairly limited area, you can use a *small broad* (preferably diffused) to provide the fill light. Larger areas need bigger *softlight* units or large multi-lamp *floodlight* fixtures. For interiors, light reflected from the ceiling or walls may supply convenient filler – although not necessarily from an appropriate angle. *Reflector boards*, too, can usefully provide filler.

Locating the fill light

Sometimes the best place for the fill light is on the camera itself, as a *camera-light*. However, there are advantages and drawbacks to this arrangement, as you will see later.

A soft light source on a lighting stand at a height of around 1 m (3–4 ft), will provide fill light which is very effective for both seated and standing performers. It tends to compensate for the downward diagonal shadows cast by hung key lights. As a rule, it is best to position the fill, so that it is some 30°–60° round from the key's direction; i.e., at 7–8 H for a key at 5 H.

Occasionally you can use strong filler on the floor beside the camera, to *under-light* a subject, and compensate for the excess modeling caused by a steep key light. (It can work wonders on ageing faces!)

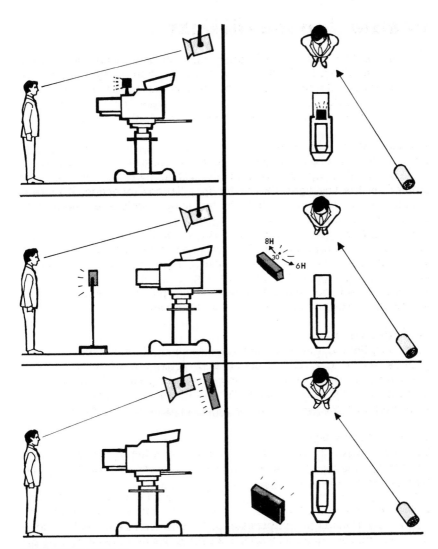

TYPES OF FILL LIGHT

Camera light
A small lightweight lamp attached to the camera may be used as fill light, or to supplement other filler. Its intensity may be controlled by a remote dimmer

Fill light on lighting stand
Soft light from a fixture on a wheeled lighting stand, is easily adjusted to suit the shot, but it may obstruct camera movement or come into shot

Hung fill light
Large soft light units may be hung, in order to keep the floor space clear. However, its vertical angle may be too steep to fill the key light's shadows effectively (e.g., under chins, brows)

Positioning the back light

Back light improves the attractiveness and clarity of the picture. It helps to model the edges of subjects and is particularly effective for translucent features. Although seldom critical, it is worth taking care to angle back light so as to bring out the subject's best features.

Arranging the back light

The usual back light is a single spotlight placed behind the subject; slightly offset towards the side opposite the key light. If it is too steep, it will strongly illuminate the tops of subjects, and this top *light* will give people bright noses and black eyes. If the vertical angle of the back light is too shallow, it can cause lens flares or the lamp may even appear in shot.

It is a good regular practice, to lower the top horizontal flap of the barndoors on back lights, to keep light out of the camera lens, and reduce the possibility of lens flares to a minimum.

Just occasionally, you can hide a back light on the ground hidden behind a subject, to lift its lower edges, or reveal edge detail.

Single back light

For large areas, a single central back light is often very effective. The shadow cast forward over the floor in front of subjects, can become part of the decorative composition. Take care though, that this shadow does not obscure important details in the shot. If, for example, someone is standing behind a table, their shadow may fall onto items they are showing the camera. To diminish this problem it may help to place a diffuser on the back light, or even use a *soft light* source instead.

Back light placed *directly behind* a subject (*dead back light*), tends to light just its *upper* edges. Offset the back light, and it will also rim-light *one-side* of the subject as well. If you offset back light by, e.g., 30°–45° (a ¾ *back*), shadows will spread *diagonally* across the foreground. This may give a rather lopsided shadow in long shots; but in practice, it is seldom a problem.

Dual back lights/double-rim lighting

If you have back lights on each side of the subject, they will provide a rim of light around it. You can create very glamorous effects this way; but take care that they are appropriate for the subject!

46

BACK LIGHT POSITIONS

Single central back light
A very effective treatment for decorative long shots. But it tends to leave the side edges of the subjects unlit

Single offset back light
Now the side edges of the subject nearer the lamp are lit, as well as the top surfaces. However, the diagonal shadows from offset back light may look unbalanced in long shots

Dual back lights – double rim lighting
This has the advantage that it illuminates both side edges of the subject. But in long shots, the crossing shadows can be distracting

47

Adjusting brightness

To create an attractive blend of light and shade you need to be able to adjust the effective brightness of lamps. You can do this in various ways.

By adjusting power
The most obvious is by using lamps of different power ratings: lower power lamps where you want less light, or there are light-toned surfaces; more powerful sources when you have a larger area to cover, or darker surroundings.

A weaker source close to the subject, may be preferable to a higher power lamp some distance away. It is easier to localize – but it may come into shot. A distant lamp has a wider light spread, but is more likely to cast shadows of cameras, slung lamps, scenery, etc, in its path.

By adjusting distance
Altering a lamp's distance from the subject, can change its virtual intensity. Most effective with soft light sources, for diffused light falls off rapidly with distance.

By adjusting spotlight focusing
When a fresnel spotlight is focused (*spotted*), its beam coverage is reduced, and the intensity increases. *Flooding* the spotlight, the light spreads and its intensity falls. So focus adjustments are a convenient method of intensity control.

By using diffusers
Diffusers of frosted plastic, spun glass, or wire mesh, cut down light to varying extents; even altering just a selected part of the light beam.

By switching bulbs
Lamp switching on multi-lamp fixtures (e.g., floodlight banks), allows you to adjust the overall light intensity. However, remember that the fewer lamps lit, the less diffuse the light will become. Some fixtures use bulbs with *dual filaments*, which can be lit separately or together, without affecting the light's color temperature.

By dimmers
Dimmers adjust a lamp's supply voltage: to alter light intensity from maximum to 'black out'; set it at a particular brightness, or fade it up/down for effect. The commonest forms of dimmer include the *thyristor* (SCR) type and *resistance* dimmers, which are available in individual units or grouped *dimmer* boards.

ADJUSTING EFFECTIVE BRIGHTNESS

Selecting power
Initially, you determine light levels
by selecting the power of the lamp
you use. A lower-wattage lamp at
the same distance will reduce
brightness – but not in proportion to
the changes in lamp power

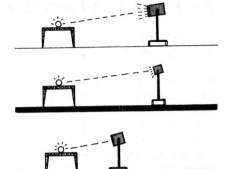

Altering lamp distance
Taking a lamp further from a subject,
will reduce the effective light level

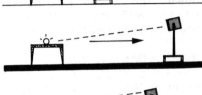

Adjusting lamp focusing
Flooding a fresnel spotlight, reduces
its light output

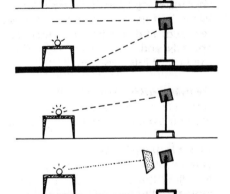

Using scrims
Placing a wire-mesh scrim, or a
diffuser over a lamp will reduce its
effective output

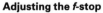

Adjusting the *f*-stop
When the camera lens is stopped
down, it effectively reduces the light
levels
If a 10 kW lamp is used at 3 m/10 ft,
with the lens set to *f*/22, the
exposure is similar to that for a
200 W lamp with the lens at *f*/1.9

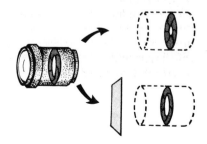

Dimmer boards

It is quite practicable to rig lamps, plug them straight to supplies, and rely on scrims/diffusers and fixture adjustment to balance their relative intensities. But if you want to be able to switch and dim supply channels, some form of dimmer board is essential. Types range from a simple switch panel, to comprehensive computerized lighting consoles with automated operation; but the underlying basics are straightforward enough.

The basic board

The simplest dimmer board consists of a row of numbered power supply circuits (channels), each with its power switch and dimmer (fader lever). A lamp patched into any of these channels can be independently switched on/off and dimmed. A group dimmer and a 'blackout' switch at the end of the row, controls them all.

Presets

Suppose we now take two independent identical versions of the basic board (now called *presets A* and *B*). On/off switches and faders for each lamp channel appear on both boards. A separate master preset switch decides which preset board is 'on air' and which on 'standby'.

You can operate any of the faders and switches, but only those for the 'on air' preset will have an immediate effect. You can, however, *set up* the corresponding channel dimmer or switches on the *other* preset in anticipation of the next time you use that preset.

If a lamp is switched on and faded up to the same level on both presets, it will remain at the same intensity whichever you use. If switched off or faded out on, e.g., preset B, it will go out when the board is turned to B preset. Full on A, and dimmed on B, its brightness alters between presets A and B.

Using the presets

The two presets allow you to make various lighting changes; e.g:

To switch or fade between groups of lamps – simply switch one lot of lamps to preset A and the other to preset B, and switch/fade between them: to alter lighting conditions (cues, lighting changes), to 'kill' lamps in one set when shooting another.

To add or subtract selected lamps from a group – put the group on one preset, and the group plus (or minus) the selected lamps on the other. Changing between presets will allow you to, e.g., fade out the action lighting, yet leave the cyc lit (people are now in silhouette). You can switch a scene from day to night, or switch 'room lights' on.

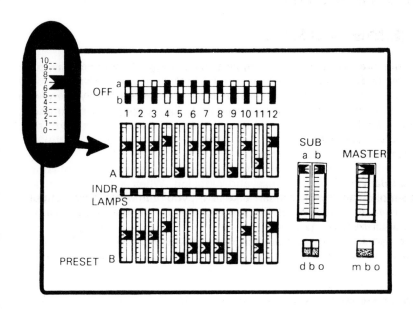

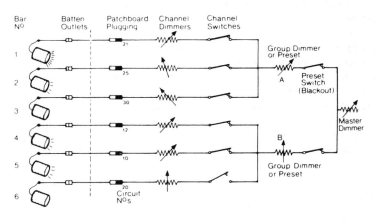

DIMMER BOARDS

Board layout

Top: Preset selection/on-off switches for each channel
Center: A and B preset faders (dimmers) with on-off indicator lamps
Sub: Independent main faders for A and B preset banks with on-off switch (DBO) for each
Master: Main fader for entire board, with main switch (MBO)

Patching

Lamps are patched as convenient, to individually adjusted circuits. These are joined in group presets, to be dimmed/switched together

51

What is lighting balance?

When you adjust the relative intensities of lamps to achieve a particular pictorial effect, you are controlling the *lighting balance*. You may simply be aiming at pleasing tonal relationships in the picture. Or you may be adjusting intensities to develop a certain mood, suggest an environment, or to direct the audience's attention to selected areas.

Adjusting lighting balance
The lighting balance begins with your choice and arrangement of lamps; their relative power, distance and diffusion. When setting lamps, and subsequently watching rehearsal pictures, you note where the brightness of individual sources needs adjustment (*trimming*), and alter them to suit the effect you have in mind.

As a general guide for most purposes: the *key light* will be strongest, fill light ⅓–½ as bright, and the *back light* ½–1 the key's intensity. Faces are often about 1½–2 as bright as their backgrounds.

Using base light
One method of lighting that originated in the early days of television is to provide a fairly strong diffuse base *light* (*foundation light*), to illuminate the entire scene. (Some people use ceiling *bounce light* for this purpose.) All other lighting is then superimposed, each lamp being made correspondingly brighter, according to the effect required.

Although this method is simple and avoids undue contrast, it can result in uninteresting characterless illumination in which modeling and texture are minimal. The setting appears 'open' and interior scenes lack any feeling of enclosure. For most purposes, such a high intensity base light is unnecessary.

Localized lighting
The widely-used technique that requires greater skill but produces superior results begins with the key lights. You begin by positioning these with care to suit the action, and adjusting their intensity for the required *f*/stop (exposure). Then you introduce fill light until shadow areas are sufficiently illuminated to reveal detail without losing modeling. You then add back light; controlling its intensity to avoid over-bright rimming. Finally, you light the background (*scene lights*, *effects lights*), and balance relative brightnesses to an appropriate level. Properly done, this technique produces attractive dynamic pictures, with a convincing impression of form and space.

Atmospheric changes
By changing the relative intensities of the various lamps lighting the setting,
you can alter the mood, the time of day, clarity

Using diffusers and scrims

Diffusers are also broadly referred to as *jellies*, *silks* or *nets*. They are made of various materials including frosted plastic sheet, spun-glass, netted fabric, even tracing paper/linen. Diffusers enable you to *soften* (*disperse*) *light*, and to *reduce the light intensity*.

Scrims, *wires* are made of wire mesh, and used to reduce the local intensity of light beam, with little diffusion.

Effectiveness

A badly-positioned diffuser on a spotlight may cause early lamp burn-out, or even a cracked lens due to overheating. Quartz lights become extremely hot! So it is advisable to insert diffuser material into a frame holder, which is clipped onto the front of a lighting fixture. This allows free air circulation and avoids the problem.

How effective a diffuser is will depend on the material used and the type of the light source. Placed over a *spotlight*, a diffuser will reduce its beam-intensity, and soften the light a little. Shadow edges will become blurred and modeling reduced. But however much you diffuse any hard source, it will never become completely shadowless. (If you rear light a large sheet of diffuser with a distant spotlight though, it does effectively become a soft light source.)

Most 'soft light' sources produce discernible shadows. Any diffusers fitted will increase light-scatter and improve their performance, at the cost of reduced output and broader light-spread.

Localized treatment

A diffuser over a lamp can reduce its effective intensity by, e.g., 5%–80% depending on the materials used. So you can actually balance light levels with considerable accuracy, without using dimmers at all. If your system has a limited number of dimmers, you can use these for effects, and rely on diffusers to adjust the intensity-balance of 'switched-only' lighting fixtures.

Instead of placing a complete diffuser ('full wire') over a spotlight, you can fix a small piece ('half wire') within the light beam. Then if, for instance, it is lighting some dark furniture in front of a light-toned wall, you can reduce the beam-strength on the wall, while leaving darker parts fully lit.

Using this principle you can provide a 'graded diffuser' with varying single, double, triple thickness, that progressively grades the light beam.

Diffusers
Diffuser medium will soften the light
from any source to some extent —
although with some loss of light. It
will help to further diffuse the
illumination from a 'soft' light source

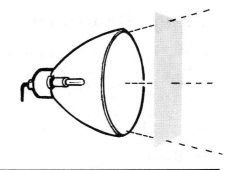

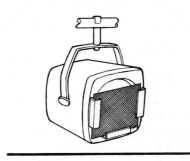

Scrim
A wire mesh scrim will cut down the
light without affecting its color
temperature

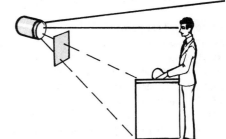

Localized light control
A piece of diffuser or a scrim can be
held in the light beam, to prevent
selected areas from being overlit

Restricting light

It is seldom sufficient to allow illumination to spread uncontrolled over the scene. Each lamp usually has a specific purpose and you will want to confine it to just this area. If light spills around there are liable to be random streaks and shadows that distract the eye and spoil the picture. Several devices are used to restrict light and control its coverage.

Barndoors
This widely used unit takes the form of a metal frame fitted with two or four separately adjustable hinged metal flaps. It clips onto the front of a spotlight, and can be rotated to position the flaps at different angles.

By adjusting one or more of the barndoor's flaps, you can ensure that a spotlight illuminates just the selected area. You can prevent the beam of one spotlight overlapping another ('doubling up'). You can restrict light to avoid ugly shadows, or stop light spilling onto nearby backgrounds.

Gobos, flags, cookies
These are all devices that interrupt the light beam in some way. A *gobo* is simply a black sheet of metal, plywood or cloth, hung up to prevent light from spilling over large areas, or to hide a lamp that is in shot. (Just to confuse matters, the term 'gobo' is also used for the metal stencil mask inserted into ellipsoidal spots, to produce a projected light pattern!)

Flags are really small gobos and come in various sizes. Held a short distance from a lamp, a flag will cut off light from a selected area more sharply than a barndoor flap. You can use a flag to cast a very precise shadow – e.g., to prevent light falling onto a particular object.

A *cookie* (*cuke*) is a metal sheet stencilled or fretted into irregular shapes. Set up in front of a spotlight, it will cast dappled light over a surface, or provide a patterned effect.

Spill rings
Spill rings are made up of a series of shallow concentric cylinders. Clipped onto the front of an internal reflector lamp and certain types of open-fronted units, they reduce light side-scatter. Some soft light units use a rectangular metal lattice that serves the same purpose.

Snoots
These cylindrical or conical tubes are sometimes clipped over spotlights, to produce a small circular 'spotlight' effect – used to pick out detail, or highlight a small area.

Barndoors
The flaps can be adjusted separately or in combination, to cut off parts of the fresnel spotlight's beam (soft-edged cut-off). Some designs use two large doors; others two large and two small

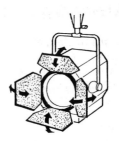

Flag
The flag is supported in front of a lighting fixture using a clamp-on rod holder, or a flexible-tube 'gooseneck'. It casts a shadow (hard or soft), or shades light off a selected area

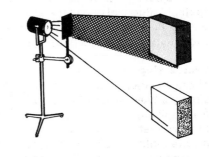

Spill rings
This clip-on attachment reduces the sideways spread of light from an open bulb, or basic lighting fixture

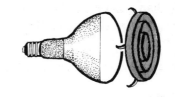

Snoot
The snoot's metal tube confines the spotlight's beam to provide a small circular area of light

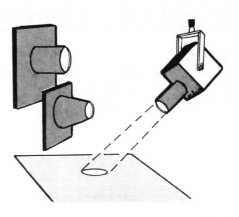

Portraiture

Most of us tend to be pretty critical when assessing pictures of people. Other subjects can be lit in almost any fashion without arousing comment, but not the human face. As people are our main subject, that means that careful portraiture techniques are a must.

Occasionally, for dramatic effect, we may light people to make them appear grotesque, aged, comic, but our usual aim is to avoid getting such effects *accidentally*!

Lighting women

By 'good portrait lighting' we invariably mean a flattering, attractive result, that minimizes the worst aspects and maximizes the best.

When lighting women it is best to avoid steep lighting from any direction, for top or side light is likely to exaggerate facial modeling. Eye-sockets become black, bags under the eyes become prominent, exaggerate wrinkles and other facial irregularities, shadows grow on the neck.

Instead, lighting should be reasonably frontal. Softened-off hard light or diffused lighting can be very effective as the key light. A woman's back light can be a little stronger than one might use for a man, to give greater definition to her hair. Double-rim backlighting can enhance hair styling. A camera light will give the eyes enlivening catchlights/eyelights.

To improve portraiture for an older woman, a low-power soft light shining upwards from just below waist level will illuminate shadows cast be the normal key and relieve neck shadows. If overdone though, this technique may flatten out modeling so that the face loses character. There is also a danger that outstretched hand shadows may fall onto her face! Except in an emergency, don't be tempted to hide ugly modeling with 'compensatory' fill light. It is better to re-position the key.

Lighting men

The general preference is for stronger, more emphatic modeling for men. So a slightly steeper key light can be most successful. Avoid strong back light; especially if a man has thin hair or is balding.

Lighting should not glamorize men. On the other hand, crude lighting looks no better on men than women. So look out for long nose shadows, black eyes, bright foreheads, glowing nose-tips, big neck shadows, shadow profiles of the head on the shoulder, bright ears, double nose shadows, and similar defects.

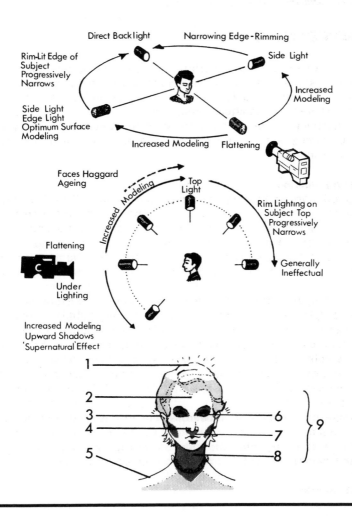

PORTRAITURE

Changing the lighting angle
Here you can see how the effect of a light changes with its angle; as it is moved higher, behind, and round the head

Typical problems in portrait lighting
Over-bright areas or ugly shadows can ruin portrait lighting

1 Bright top to the head
2 Bright forehead
3 Bright ears
4 Bright nose
5 Hot shoulders

6 Black eyes
7 Long nose shadow
8 Black 'bib' neck shadow
9 Excessive facial modeling

In this example, 1, 2, 3, 4, 5 are caused by steep back light. 2, 6, 7, 8, 9 result from a steep bright frontal key light

Lighting a single person

Of course we can't lay down strict rules for portrait lighting. But there are reliable working principles from which your own interpretations can grow.

Ideally, you would choose lighting angles that 'correct' or minimize any less attractive features (e.g. deep set eyes, protruding ears, etc.). Inconsiderate lighting can draw attention to or exaggerate them. There may be times when you have to 'light a chair' without seeing the person on-camera beforehand. Then you apply a regular 'three-point' treatment, based on where they are probably facing (perhaps using a stand-in), and make last-minute changes as necessary.

Full face

When lighting a face, you must always think in three-dimensions. A lamp's effect is influenced by both how steep it is (*vertical angle – V*), and how far round the subject it is positioned (*H*) relative to the camera. The clock-face indicator helps you to pinpoint the lamp's position.

The *key light* can be placed to the left or the right of the camera. Which you choose, should depend on the inherent balance of proportions of the person's features. In practice, it is often determined by production mechanics; e.g., where he/she is going to move next.

The figures opposite show you typical positions for the key, fill and back lights. When the key is only slightly offset (around 6 H), the nose shadow will be small, and the modeling slight. Narrower horizontal angles are more youthening (flattening), and may need less fill light (at a height of level to + 20° (+2 V)).

Moving the key round 45° (towards 8 H or −8 H) the nose shadow grows longer, until it links up with the cheek shadow, and forms a triangle of light. Some faces look dynamic under an angled key, others look lopsided!

The *back light* should usually be on the opposite side from the key direction. Take care that it is not offset too much, or it will probably overlight one side of the face, causing a bright nose, black eye, and a forward ear shadow!

Profile

As a rough guide, as the head turns away from the lens the key should follow the nose direction ('lighting along the nose line'). If modeling is too slight, take the key further round towards the back of the person. If the nose shadow is too pronounced, move the key towards the nose-line or lower it.

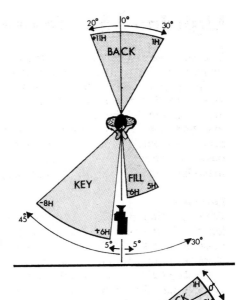

Facing the camera – full face
Here you see typical directions for
three-point treatment, when lighting
someone facing the camera

The offset head
As the head is turned, the optimum
light directions for good portraiture
change. Here are the directions for a
¾-frontal position, and a profile.

Vertical lighting angle
The height and vertical angles of the
key and back lights should be
chosen carefully for the best results

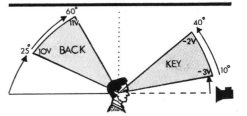

61

Lighting two people

As you might expect, there are various schools of thought here. Each of the techniques we look at has its particular artistic or practical advantages. Choose the approach that satisfies your own taste – and your circumstances.

Light direction
Upstage cross lighting – Here the keys and back lights are placed on the far side of the people from the camera (i.e., 'upstage'). This regularly used method avoids shadows of the subjects or a sound boom falling onto the background. Because the key lights do not illuminate the background, this can be lit separately, so giving greater lighting control.
Frontal cross lighting – Particularly where space and equipment are limited, this approach has the advantage that the key lights also illuminate the background behind the speakers, so avoiding the need for extra lamps.
Aligned lighting – This is an arrangement that has the merit of maintaining the same light direction in intercut shots.

Dual purpose lamps
Ideally, we would like to light people quite *individually*. But this is often impracticable for various reasons. You may not have enough lighting fixtures. There may be insufficient space to rig them. The usual dilemma is that people are too close together to light them separately. The key, back, or fill for one person would spill onto his neighbor. Each person would shadow the other. Any attempt to restrict or steepen lighting, would simply degrade the portraiture.

If you cannot reposition people, one solution is a *communal* lighting set-up. This takes the form of three-point treatment, with a single frontal key light covering both people, a single back light, and shared fill light.

Where people are angled to the camera, a better arrangement uses *dual-purpose* lamps; in which each person's key falls on the neighbor as back light. This is fine provided both people need similar light intensities. However, you will generally find that you need lower intensity back light for fair hair, bald heads, straight hair, light-toned clothes, bare shoulders; while for black hair, curly hair, black clothing, velvets, it will need to be stronger. Key strengths, too, will vary with skin tones.

Clearly any communal or dual-purpose lighting involves a certain amount of luck. But you can often improve the lighting balance by using pieces of diffuser to reduce the amount of key or back light falling on an individual.

LIGHTING TWO PEOPLE

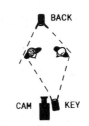

Communal lighting
When the camera is shooting straight-on to the action, a frontal key light may be the most economical method of lighting two people

Upstage cross-lighting
Keys and back light are located beyond a line joining the two people

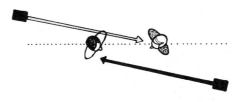

Frontal cross lighting
Here the keys and backlights are placed on the camera side of a line joining the two people

Aligned lighting
Key and back lights are aligned diagonally across the performers

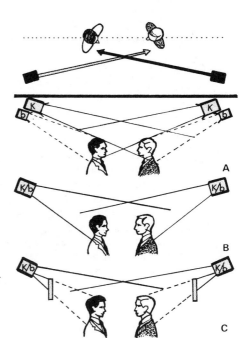

Dual purpose lamps
Methods of arranging back lights for two subjects:

A Separate treatments
B Shared key/back lights
C Local back light reduction

Lighting a group

'Groups' come in all shapes and sizes. At one end of the scale we have three or four people sitting in a ring of chairs or behind desks in a quiz show. At the other, one meets larger groups regularly as audiences, choirs, orchestras, even crowds.

In most cases, lighting treatment is straightforward but where the group is arranged at different levels (e.g., on a series of elevated areas), it can be more difficult to isolate them, or to avoid those behind cutting off any back light from those in front.

Individual treatment
With groups of up to about half a dozen people, it is often quite practicable to light each person individually.

Provided people are spaced about 0.5 m/1.5 ft apart (e.g., a person's width), and you use closely barndoored key and back lights, you can isolate and adjust lighting to suit the characteristics of each speaker. Communal fill light is necessary, as soft light cannot be restricted to cover individuals.

Communal treatment
Where several people are grouped or standing in line, you can often use a single communal key light, and either a single or dual back lights. Again, fill light will be shared.

How many people you can cover with a single spotlight will depend on its maximum spread (e.g., 60°), its distance ('throw'), and its light output. You may find that a group six wide and six deep is a typical maximum.

Subdivision
When dealing with a continuous mass of people, such as a *studio audience*, the best technique is to split the gathering into a series of side-by-side areas, and give each a key and back light, with communal fill light. Using barndoors, you limit the amount of overlap. (It is really a form of area lighting – *sectional keys*.) Although you might be able to use one powerful key to cover the entire group (e.g., an HMI arc), this will give you less control than a series of separate keys.

Some large groups are readily subdivided into sections or *sub-groups*. When lighting an orchestra, for instance, you might light strings, woodwind, percussion, etc., each with their own group keys and back lights, while soloists and the conductor are lit separately. Although it is advisable to keep light levels and contrast reasonably similar throughout a group, video adjustments can usually compensate for unavoidable variations.

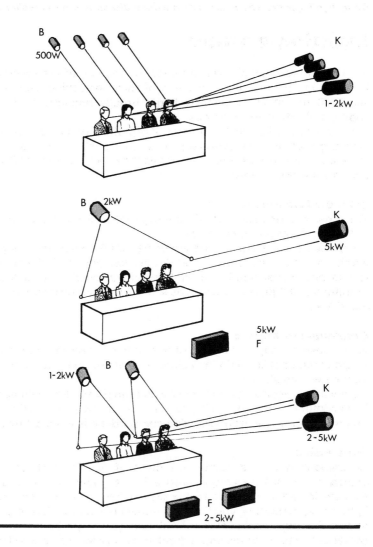

LIGHTING A GROUP

Individual treatment
Here each person in a typical quiz-show group is lit individually. The fill light will usually be communal, for it cannot be localized. The actual power required for lighting fixtures will depend on distances, lens stops, camera sensitivity, etc. but these are typical

Communal treatment
Here the same three-point treatment covers the whole group. (Its intensity and direction may not suit them all)

Sub-division
Here the group is divided into pairs, who share a key and back light

65

People talking – typical set-ups

No measured lighting set-up can be more than a guide. After all, two people can switch on the same set of lamps and by slight readjustments get substantially different results. Alterations in the lighting balance alone can change the entire pictorial effect.

Developing techniques

For most of us, the initial problem is in knowing how to begin. As you gain experience in lighting, confidence grows; but those preliminary steps can be pretty daunting – especially when lighting *people* for the first time. Fewer subjects are more critical than the human face. Everyone is ready to make judgments.

When lighting an *object*, you can experiment impartially as you seek to get the best effect. But lighting a *person* is a responsibility. You have a sense of obligation. They are often waiting while you light them, and depending on you to make them look attractive.

The diagrams here are essentially *guides*. They will give you an idea how you can start to light such regular, every-day set-ups; especially when time is pressing. Your particular circumstances will differ – but not in essentials.

Measuring lamp positions

Creative individuals are rightly suspicious of any 'statistics'. But it is far better to set out with a plan of campaign than to spend endless time in disappointing experiment.

There can be no hard-and-fast 'rules'. Lighting fixtures vary in their design and efficiency. Much depends on how you use them. For example:

- You can take a 500 watt back light, and spot it so that it is as strong (over a limited area) as a fully-flooded 2-kilowatt lamp.
- The key (or the fill light) might illuminate the background sufficiently, so that no extra lighting is needed there.
- If the key is very frontal (i.e., near the camera), you may need no fill light at all.
- If the camera is working with a large lens aperture (e.g., *f*/1.9), or is particularly sensitive, you will need noticeably lower light levels than when using a smaller stop (e.g., *f*/8).

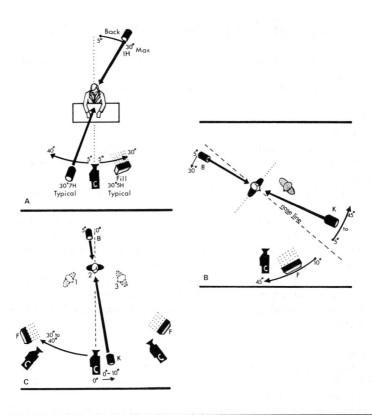

PEOPLE TALKING

A Announcer set-up
Typical lamp positions, using lamp heights around 2.5 to 3 m/8 to 10 ft

	Sitting	Standing
Key light (1–2 kW)	2.5–3.6 m	1.3–2 m
	8–12 ft	4–7 ft
Fill light (1–2 kW)	1.5–2.5 m	1.5–2.5 m
(at height 1.3 to 2 m/4 to 7 ft)	5–8 ft	5–8 ft
Back light (1 kW–500 W)	1.5–2.5 m	1–1.5 m
	5–8 ft	3–5 ft

B Interview set-up for two people
Lamp distances as in **A** (height 2.5 to 3 m/8–10 ft).
Angles measured from the nose line (at right angles to the body).
The other person is lit with an identical mirror-image set-up

C Interview set-up for three people
Persons 1 and 3 lit as for a two-person interview (see **B**). Central person lit as in **A**, with a central key

67

Problem occasions

Even the most straightforward production can present you with lighting problems that do not have obvious solutions. However, with a little anticipation, you can usually adopt an approach that will get satisfactory results. Here are some regular examples.

A head turns

When someone's head turns through a right angle, the lighting that was successful for the original head direction, may not look so attractive for its new position.

For instance, if you light a *profile* shot 'along the nose' (3 H or 9 H) the modeling will be effective. But if the head then turns to face the camera the same source has now become *side light*, causing the face to be edge-lit and unattractively bisected. The best compromise here is to place the key at a mid-point between the two positions (45°).

As a rule of thumb, we can say that where a head turns *away* from the key, portraiture generally deteriorates. Where it turns *towards* the key, the result is quite satisfactory – it may even be improved.

Quite simple situations may need careful lighting treatment. For example, when a group of people sit in a horseshoe arrangement, a central key that looks fine when shooting from the front may not suit cross-shooting cameras. Instead, you may find it preferable to cross-fade between separate angled keys to suit different camera viewpoints.

Positions near walls

When someone is standing near a wall, you can either light him 'along the wall' as in Figure 2A, or use a 'straight-on' key, as in Figure 2B – depending on which direction he is facing, and the position of the camera. If the person turns, or talks to someone else, an 'auxiliary key' may help matters.

Where two people stand face-to-face near walls, don't be tempted to squirt light down onto them from the wall top. The vertical illumination will simply produce unattractive 'black eyes' and 'hot' tops to heads (*top light*).

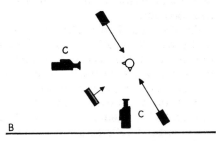

1 The head turns

A. The lighting set-up suitable for one head position may not suit another

On **Cam 1** the full face is well lit, but the profile flatly illuminated
On **Cam 2** the head is unattractively bisected with light

B One lighting set-up may suit both cameras sufficiently for full-face shots

C Another set-up suits full face and profiles on both cameras

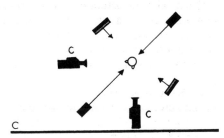

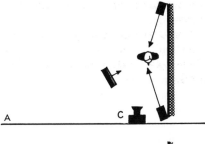

2 Positions near walls

A *Lighting along walls.* Here the hard light does not light the wall surface

B *Upstage key light,* supplemented by an auxiliary key if the subject turns to camera, or for a two-shot

69

Anticipating trouble

Although it is in everyone's interest to plan and rehearse action before shooting, this is not always practicable. So you have to try to ensure that your lighting treatment allows for the unexpected. Even where retakes are possible there may be few opportunities for extensive lighting corrections.

Preliminary checks
After you have completed your lighting, it is a good idea to spend a few minutes checking it over. Look out for those odd defects you overlooked when setting the lamps; such as distracting shadows, leak light on walls, unevenness in background lighting, hotspots, 'dirty light'.

Whenever you can, try to check out the initial effects of your lighting on camera before rehearsals begin. Even a brief shot or two will give you valuable clues to the lighting balance. You will be able to see if parts of the background are too strongly lit, or need additional lighting. An ugly shadow that you have overlooked when setting lamps, may be very prominent on camera.

If the actual performers are not available, take a look at 'stand-ins' sitting or standing at the planned positions. Clothing and appearance will differ, and you will need to interpret – especially if a swarthy bearded giant in a sweater is substituting for the eventual diminutive blond in an off-shoulder dress. But this check can still be a great help.

Critical lighting
The trick is to avoid making lighting too critical; so that it only works if the person sits perfectly still at the exact angle.
- If the key light is too restricted, the talent may move in and out of it. A person may move into a neighbor's lights.
- When the back light is steep, it will illuminate the nose and forehead, particularly if the head is tilted back.
- When someone looks downwards, their key light effectively steepens and their eye sockets fall into shadow.
- If there is a chance that a person will be looking away from the expected direction (e.g., to watch a nearby picture monitor), take this into account when choosing the key direction; or even rig a second key light as a 'standby'.
- When lighting an area for action, do not assume that performers will keep within a limited lit section. In the excitement of the moment, you may well find that dancers come forward out of the light; or that a speaker does not walk to the marked spot on the floor but stands off-key ('off his marks')!

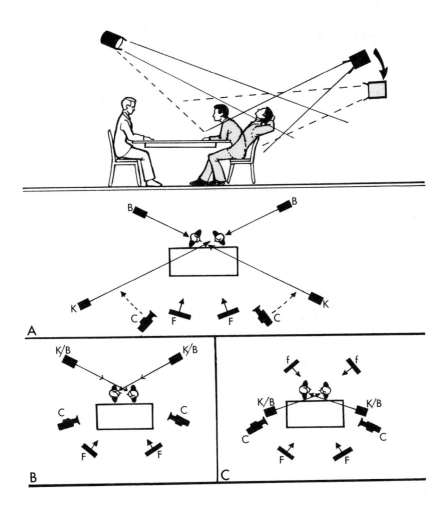

ANTICIPATING TROUBLE

Fidgety performers

Don't make lighting angles too critical. When the person on the right leans forward, he moves out of both the key and back lights. When he leans back, the steep back light emphasizes facial modeling. The broken lines show improved versions

Taking precautions (A)

The director *angled* the seats to suit the shots he required. But the talent unexpectedly turned to face each other. Now the upstage side of their faces were underlit. The cameras were repositioned to correct the shots, but what could be done to improve the lighting treatment? The solutions were either **(B)** to cross fade to different key directions; or **(C)** to fade up standby fill-lights **(f)**

People moving

If someone remains still, your lighting can be tailor-made to suit their particular needs. For example, you can compensate for a high forehead by shading the key light to make it less prominent. The more they move around, the less opportunity there is for exact lamp positioning. But at the same time, there is also less chance for the audience to see any imperfections in the lighting treatment!

There are situations where the only way you can hope to light a moving person effectively, is to follow him/her with a spotlight, hand-held light, or a camera light (e.g., when news-gathering). This may be effective enough, but you really need much more controllable techniques.

Individual areas

If someone is standing beside a table, then walks over to a wall map, you can provide separate three-point lighting at each static postition. Whether you arrange a key and back light for the walk-thro' area (i.e., 'light the walk'), rely on spill light, or leave it in darkness, will depend on the nature of the production.

Subdivided areas

Another approach to movement, is to break the total acting area into a series of smaller *sub-areas*. Each is lit with an appropriate three-point set-up. Now when *anyone* enters at the door, or stands by the fireplace, or sits by the window, they are suitably lit by that sub-area's lamps.

If there are various sorts of action in the same area, each requiring its own lighting treatment, you may be able to cross-fade (or switch) from one set-up to another while the camera is shooting a different part of the scene, or even make the changes surreptitiously, during the action.

Overall treatment

The simplest way of lighting action within an area, is to provide an overall pattern of light; a 'giant three-point approach' that you hope will suit the action from various camera viewpoints. You can modify or augment this broad treatment as necessary. Although this is the least flexible technique, it is really the only practical approach when the action is very widespread, when movement is unpredictable, or when there is insufficient equipment for more specific treatment.

If you learn that you have a dance group to light, but the director has only a vague idea which shots he is going to take, this is the solution!

PEOPLE MOVING

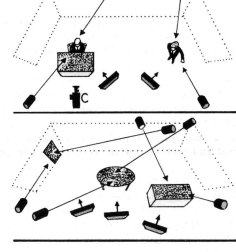

Individual areas
Each person's position is lit separately

Subdivided areas
Each part of the setting is lit for any performer *in that* area

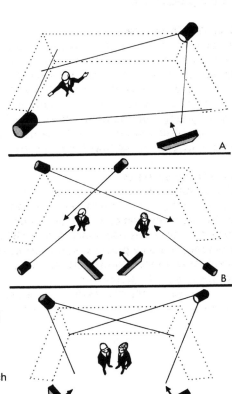

Total treatment
A *An overall* three-point scheme to accommodate action
B *Dual-key* lighting splits the total area into two, each with its own three-point treatment
C *Soft frontal* area lighting, in which two ¾ back lights provide hard modeling for cross shooting cameras

73

Frustrated lighting

You will meet situations where, however much you try, the lighting remains unsatisfactory. You cannot position lamps where they are really needed. Sometimes other people can help, if you explain the difficulty.

Position
Most settings (and locations) have problem areas that you can only light from certain directions; e.g., under low ceilings, beneath deep arches, or in confined spaces (e.g., cupboards). You can usually illuminate them in some fashion, but is the light direction appropriate for the subject? If the result is unacceptable, it may be necessary to reposition the action, or alter the camera angle.

Head angle
Performers can often help you if you let them know the problem. Someone standing with a half-lit face will happily turn towards the key light if you explain. If a downward tilted head causes 'black eyes' and harsh modeling, it is easier to tell them than try to reposition the key!

Shadows
Mutual shadowing: When people stand close together, one will often shadow the other. If this is pointed out to them, the performers themselves can clear the shadow by a slight head movement, or by re-angling their bodies. The alternative would be to move the key direction, and this could upset other shots.
Camera shadows: When a camera gets very close, its shadow may fall onto the subject. Either raise the key light, or have the camera work further away, using a narrower lens angle.
Scenery: When organizing lighting treatment, check whether scenery is likely to cast distracting shadows onto performers, or to ruin a scenic effect (e.g., tree shadows on a sky backdrop). The lighting or the scenery may need to be adjusted. Hanging objects (cloths, chandeliers) may block off the key light for an important acting position.

Simultaneous contrast/spatial induction
When a person's background looks over-bright, this can be due to an optical illusion known as *simultaneous contrast* (*spatial induction*) causing tonal contrasts to appear exaggerated. It may also be aggravated by the person's key light falling onto the background, and over-lighting it. The solution may be to light person and background separately, to adjust the camera angle to exclude the bright area, or to change the background tone.

Tipping the head

As the head is tipped down, the key light's effective vertical angle steepens, and the modeling becomes harsher and exaggerated. Downward shadows grow longer

Clearing shadows

You can often avoid one person's shadow falling on another (A), by having them move sideways (B), or pivot round (C)

75

Changing camera positions

It is obvious enough when you stop and think about it, but the effective 'direction' of light always depends on the camera's viewpoint. Light an object with a single lamp and from one camera position its illumination will be *frontal*, from another it becomes *side light*, while from another it is *back light*. As you saw earlier, each light direction has a different effect; so the subject's appearance can change noticeably on switching between viewpoints. From one position the subject can look dark with a bright rim; from another, flatly lit with a frontal key! How do you cope with changes of this sort?

General solutions

You could use a ring of lamps, lighting the subject from all directions, so that whatever the camera's position, the subject remained lit. The result would be innumerable shadows, each lamp's modeling being diluted by the others. The overall result would be a picture lacking crisp firm definition.

It is far better to follow the more systematic approaches we discussed earlier, based on three-point lighting techniques. You can use a form of area lighting similar to that for a moving person; modified where necessary to improve particular shots (e.g., by adding an extra localized key or fill light).

Preferred position

In this approach, you ensure that the lighting provides good portraiture for the more important camera position (e.g., for close-ups), even if it looks rather less effective from another direction (e.g., for long shots).

Dual set-up

Here lighting angles are carefully chosen to suit both camera directions equally well. The arrangement in the example opposite could be used either for a person who turns over a wide angle from one camera to another, or for two people in conversation.

Specific solutions

The final obvious way of arranging lighting to suit various camera positions is to have a different lighting set-up for each, and to switch or cross-fade between them. Provided this can be done unobtrusively (and you have the facilities) this method can work well. However, there is always the chance that lighting continuity will be upset when intercutting a succession of shots. A variation on this method is to record *long shots* first, then re-light the subject before shooting *close shots*.

CHANGING CAMERA POSITIONS

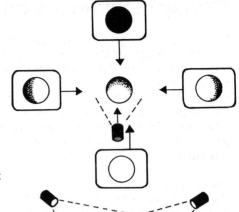

Altering the viewpoint
The effect of a particular lamp will
change with the camera's viewpoint

Area lighting
Here the area lighting set-up may
suit both positions

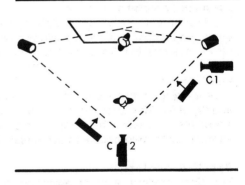

Preferred position
The set-up that provides the best
results for **Cam 1** is still acceptable
for **Cam 2's** shot

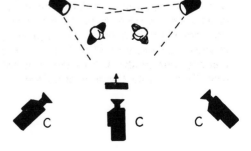

Dual set-up
The localized lighting may suit both
subjects well from all camera
positions

Portable lamps

As the video camera has become lighter and more mobile, there has been an increasing need to carry some form of illumination with it. This takes two forms; a small lighting fixture attached to the camera itself; or a separate hand-held unit.

The camera light

In the studio, a lamp of, e.g., 100–350 watts is often attached to the camera to provide:

- 'Eye-lights', to reflect in the eyes as catch-lights.
- Frontal fill-light, to reduce the key's modeling.

The lamp may be dimmer controlled or manually adjusted, and is usually fitted with scrim/diffuser to adjust the light intensity and soften the illumination.

On location, a lamp fixed to the camera can provide a key light or fill light for the action. A dichroic filter can be attached when shooting in daylight. The camera light is usually powered from the camera's supplies. A *battery-powered* lamp offers greater mobility, but for a limited duration. (A 250 W/30 V may run for 30 minutes, while a 350 W lamp would only last for about 20 minutes.) When the system is run from a utility/mains supply, an *a.c. adaptor* will be needed, but the lighting time is no longer limited; although the trailing supply cable may be rather restrictive.

The camera light's great advantage is that it goes with the camera, wherever it moves, and does not require the aid of a second person. It provides a flattering key or fill light. But there are drawbacks. It will not necessarily illuminate all the camera can see. Its light may not reach distant parts of the action, although people nearer the camera may be dazzled or overlit. Its coverage often falls off at the edges of the shot. You may find on zooming in to details that they are underlit. The picture may reveal light sweeping across the scene as the camera pans in a long shot. There is also a likelihood that light will be reflected in spectacles, shiny/glossy backgrounds as a strong white blob ('kickback').

Hand-held light ('Sun gun')

If a small hand-held lightweight lamp is operated by a separate person, it not only relieves the cameraman of extra weight, but allows the unit to be angled for the best results. The lamp can be held high to provide better modeling, and the illuminated area can be held constant.

Power ratings for hand-held units range from e.g., 250–1000 watts (battery or a.c. powered), with fan-cooling to avoid over-heating. Both regular and overrun bulbs are used.

PORTABLE LAMPS

The camera light
A small lamp attached to the camera is useful as a mobile key light or filler

Hand-held lamp
A hand-held lamp operated by an assistant has the advantages that it can be pointed more accurately, and kept steady on the subject when the camera moves. It can also be larger, and of higher power

79

Lighting on a shoestring

There will be times when for one reason or another you have to attempt the 'impossible' and light with inadequate resources. Let's look at some possible solutions to this dilemma.

Just a single lamp

Even a *single lamp* may be sufficient in unlit surroundings if you are lighting:

- A fairly restricted flat area. (Use it as a frontal key.)
- A situation where the camera concentrates on a subject's outline (use it as back light); or a side profile (use it as side or ¾-frontal key).
- Sihouetted subjects. (Light just the background.)
- Translucent subjects. (Use it as back light.)
- A situation where a pool of light is appropriate.

You may be able to augment your single lamp by reflecting some of its illumination with a reflector board faced with metal-foil. For example, a back light can be reflected to provide a supplementary key light or fill light. A key may be reflected as back light or filler.

Daylight can help

If you are lighting an interior, where there is sunlight coming through a window, you may have several choices. (Your lamp will need blue color correction.)

- If you decide to use the sunlight as a *key*, reposition the subject if necessary. Your single lamp may serve as back light, fill light or background lighting.
- With your lamp as the key, use the daylight to provide fill light, back light, or background lighting (direct or reflected).

Remember, a metal-foil faced reflector will provide strong *hard* reflected light (and will even reflect daylight alone, when the sun is not shining). A white-faced board will reflect the sun's light as diffuse illumination.

If the sunlight is from the wrong direction, or you need a further light source, you can also use a *relay reflector* to alter the reflected light path.

Using two lamps

Two lamps will increase your opportunities considerably. Not only can you try variations on the above, but with care, you can combine functions. For instance, when cross-lighting two people in an interview, the lamp that provides back light for person A, can key person B *and* then light the background behind them. The second lamp is used similarly from the opposite direction.

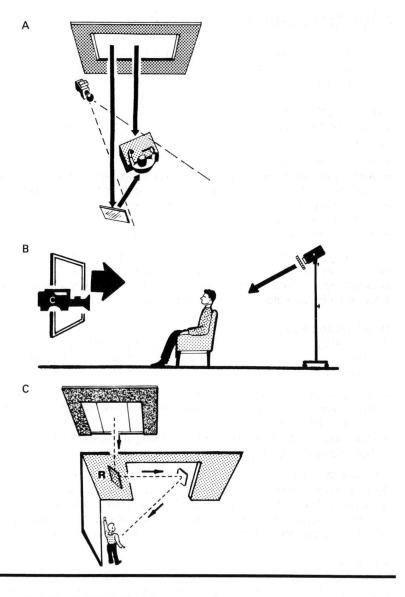

LIGHTING ON A SHOESTRING

Augmenting daylight
A You can light the subject with direct daylight (as the key light), using a metal-foil faced reflector board, to provide reflected daylight as back light
B The direct daylight can be used to key the subject, while a single lamp (blue filtered) is used as a back light
C Where the direction of the sun is unsuitable for direct or reflected lighting, you may be able to use a *relay reflector to redirect it*

Demonstrations – typical set-ups

Video is an excellent medium for demonstrations of all kinds: from classroom experiments to equipment sales; from cooking techniques to project presentations.

The demonstration area

You will probably begin with a straight 'three-point lighting' treatment. A single key light will often be sufficient for both the demonstrator and the items he is showing. But when the subject being demonstrated is at all complex (e.g., close shots of clock mechanisms), these items may need additional lighting. (A camera light will probably improve the situation.)

Some subjects are easier to light separately if the demonstrator stands beside the subject rather than behind it. You can use a small strong spotlight to emphasize a particular feature of a display, but remember, if the demonstrator puts his hand into this area, it will be considerably overlit! (Use a pointer!)

Small details are often clearer if the subject is specially lit; e.g., edge-lit coins or assay marks on silver, or fossils lit with ultraviolet light. It is better to shoot such close-ups separately, and edit them into the program afterwards.

Positioning the demonstrator's key light

Because people tend to look downwards during demonstrations, it is best to keep the key light at a reasonably shallow vertical angle (say, 30°, i.e., 2V). If you make it flatter (between 3V and 2V), you may dazzle the demonstrator, or prevent his reading any cue sheets (reminder boards) or prompters near the camera. There is the possibility, too, of 'kick-back' from light-toned or specular reflections from glossy surfaces.

When the key light is at a shallow angle, you may have trouble with the camera's shadow falling onto objects as it gets in close – especially if it elevates to look down into them.

If you make the key light steep, portraiture deteriorates; particularly when the demonstrator bends forward or looks down. It can also be more difficult to avoid shadows from any overhead mirror.

Wall Displays

Various kinds of wall displays, such as maps, charts, or diagrams, are a familiar part of many demonstrations. Here you need to take care that the person's shadow does not fall across the display. You may need to check in advance, where he is going to stand, and whether he is left- or right-handed.

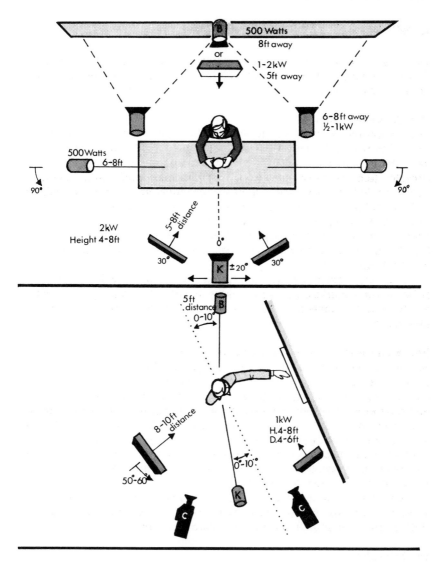

TYPICAL SET-UPS

The demonstration table
In this example, the key is central, with fill light offset to suit cross-shooting cameras. If a sound boom is used, angle the key to throw shadows out of shot.
Back light may be hard (barndoored off the table), or a soft light source

The wall display
This may be a wall-mounted map, chart, screen, chalkboard, etc. The main problem is to avoid the person's shadow falling onto the subject (from the key or back light), while achieving good portraiture

Demonstrations – lighting problems

A demonstration can be an exacting exercise, for the lighting that produces good portaiture, may not provide the best results for the subject being demonstrated. Here are some important points to look out for:

Potential problems

- You may find it helpful to barndoor the main key to restrict it to the demonstrator. You can then light the items on the table separately with other localized lighting at the front and side of the table.
- If the demonstration bench or table has a covered-in front, take care that the frontal key does not over-light it. Shade it off with a bottom barndoor flap, scrim or diffuser.
- Check that objects on the table do not shadow each other unduly.
- Are there any distracting specular reflections? Try angling or repositioning the troublesome objects. Spraying with dulling spray ('anti-flare') may sufficiently reduce reflections. Perhaps you can hide the shiny surface, by placing another item in front of it. Occasionally, the best solution is to remove the offending item until it is actually needed. Sometimes it can even be necessary to 'kill' the lamp that is causing the specular reflection for certain shots – or even change the lighting.
- When the camera is shooting large shiny surfaces, try to keep the number of reflected light sources to a minimum. Rather than have the spotty effect of a number of separate reflected lamps, try to arrange soft light sources as a continuous group which reflects as a block of light. Because curved shiny surfaces can reflect lamps from all over the studio, switch off any in other nearby areas that are not actually being used for the shot.
- Back light will cast forward shadows. On a table full of objects they may not be at all obvious. But even a single shadow falling onto a plain surface (e.g., a horizontal map) is distracting. You can often avoid shadows by tightly barndooring the back light. Soft back light may be the answer – but it will spread around, and be difficult to control.
- If a large mirror is hung over the table to provide overhead shots (the camera shoots via the mirror), it is possible to light items on the table by directing a spotlight into the mirror.
- Multiple shadows can be very confusing, especially on wall displays, so check for any overlapping keys.

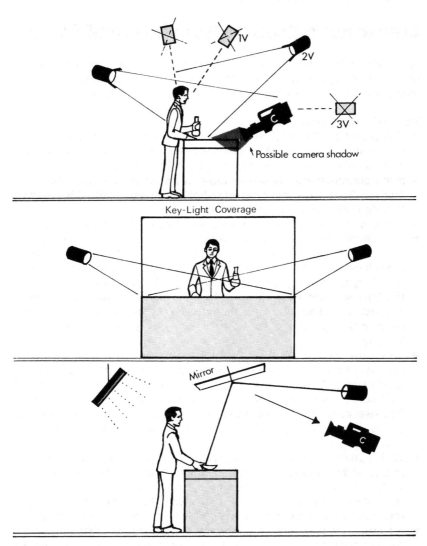

Key-Light Coverage

Possible camera shadow

Mirror

PROBLEMS

Lamp heights
Because demonstrators tend to look downwards, it is best to avoid steep key lights. However, if the key's vertical angle is too shallow, close cameras may throw shadows onto the table

Localized lighting
Sometimes it is better to confine the frontal key-light to the demonstrator, and to provide side keys to edge-light subjects on the table

Overhead shots
An overhead mirror is often used to look down into subjects being demonstrated (e.g. during cookery demonstrations). To get 'overhead' lighting into the subjects, reflect a key via the mirror

85

Lighting for clarity

Occasionally we rely on softened detail and obscuring shadows to create a particular dramatic effect. But for most types of production *clarity* is essential.

Tone, size and distance
If you stop the lens down, this will considerably increase the *depth of field*, and everything in the scene will look sharply defined. But *deep focus* can be a mixed blessing. When *everything* in the shot is sharp, there is a tendency for planes to merge, producing a flat overall effect. On the other hand, when the focused depth is shallow, subjects tend to stand out clearly against an unsharp background.

You can modify the impression of solidity and distance in the picture in various ways, through selective lighting.

- Light toned planes appear larger and more distant.
- Graded tones take the eye from darker to lighter areas.
- Lighter tones convey spaciousness; while darker tones create a closed-in feeling.
- Outside a window, light tones suggest distance beyond.

Tonal differentiation
A subject is liable to appear to merge with its background unless there is a good tonal contrast between them – even when they are of different colors.

A light-toned subject tends to stand out from its background more clearly than a dark-toned one. (The exception is very dark against very light tones.) Dark-toned areas tend to lose modeling and detail. Over-bright backgrounds can distract.

Back light can improve the outline clarity, particularly if the surface is uneven (fur, feathers, foliage), or the subject is translucent. But remember, excess backlight can cheapen a subject, making it look artificial, gaudy, showy.

Physical character
We recognize the objects around us, by their characteristic shapes and surface features: rough, smooth, shiny, matte, undecorated, deco-rated . . . . If lighting doesn't reveal those particular features, these objects will not look completely 'real' in the picture. They may even be unrecognizable! A textured wall can look absolutely smooth if flatly lit. Under even lighting, a ball may look like a plain disc.

Shadows falling across a surface reveal its contours, but they can also obscure its details. Light reflecting on an oil painting may show us the glossy nature of the canvas, but prevent our seeing the picture itself! When 'painting with light' we can easily ruin clarity.

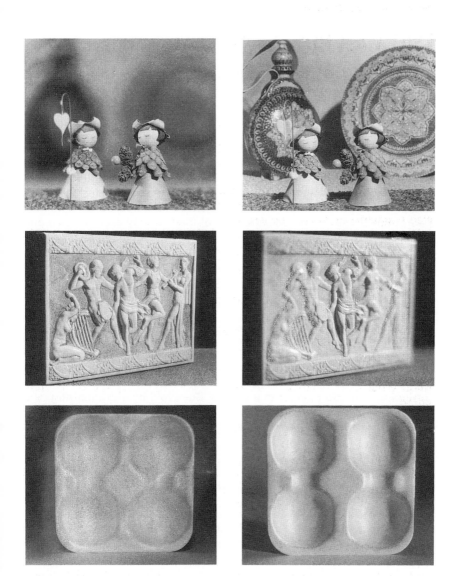

LIGHTING FOR CLARITY

Depth of field
By restricting the depth of field, you can eliminate distracting background details, and concentrate the audience's attention

Where you want overall clarity, *maximum* depth of field is essential

Form and texture
When this molded surface is lit frontally, the picture conveys little of its form and texture. An angled key gives a far better idea of the actual contours

Pictorial lighting

Of course, there are no magic rules for creating 'eye appeal'. But there are certainly techniques that make pictures more attractive – and others that are best avoided.

Backgrounds

Walls look better if gradually shaded, leaving them darker at the top. This helps to create a sense of 'enclosure' for interiors, and improves the tonal contrast between faces and background. A sharp light cut-off on walls, usually looks unnatural. Backgrounds that are much brighter at the *top* usually result in unattractively unbalanced pictures. Bright flatly-lit backgrounds with no particular center of interest may appear 'open and spacious'. But they can also look blank and very dull unless they happen to be strongly colored. Check for any spotlight accidentally edge-lighting backgrounds, exaggerating any irregularities. Light scraping along cycloramas, backdrops, etc., can reveal distracting wrinkles and unevenness.

Shadows

Avoid shadows falling onto photo backgrounds, or painted scenic backgrounds, that can spoil any illusion of solidity or perspective. When lighting interiors, look out for those accidental eye-catching shadows cast by decorative wall-light fittings, chandeliers, etc. Shadowy areas can be intriguing and add interest to a picture. But avoid over-dramatizing, and creating deep shadows that leave your audience frustrated – feeling that they are missing important details.

Light patterns

While a *single* decorative shadow can be very attractive, avoid having too many. *Complicated shadow patterns* take one's eye from the action, particularly if they happen to be distorted or incomplete. *Uncoordinated light patterns* scattered over a background are distracting, and are liable to appear as odd random shapes in closer shots. *Defocused soft-edged patterns* can produce some very beautiful abstract effects. *Irregular patterns* can break up an otherwise plain and uninteresting background – e.g., dappled leaf shadows on walls. *Geometric patterns* must usually be sharp, and projected accurately; any distortion or partial defocusing is particularly obvious. *Slowly-moving indistinct pattern shapes* can be extremely attractive. But *fast regular movements* of sharp light patterns soon appear very mechanical.

PICTORIAL LIGHTING

Background shading
A shaded background generally provides a more attractive effect than a plain even surface

Hard-edged shading produces an artificial, segmented effect, and is only used occasionally

Complete shadows
If you are making a decorative feature of shadows, make sure that they are not broken up or cut off by scenery

Shadow effects

Shadows stimulate the imagination. You can use them to create an atmosphere simply, effectively and economically. Shadows can reveal information, showing us what would otherwise be hidden from our viewpoint. They can create suspense and mystery.

Types of shadow

Basically, you can produce shadow effects in three ways:

1. *Cast shadows*. This is the most obvious method. You simply place an object in the directional light from a 'hard' source.
2. *Projected shadows*. Here the image of a gobo (metal stencilled sheet) or a slide is projected onto the background using an optical projector – *ellipsoidal spotlight* (*profile spot*).
3. *Silhouetted shadow*. You can create a silhouette by placing an unlit subject against a brightly lit background.

Alternatively, you can cast a subject's shadow onto the back of a translucent rear-lit screen.

Effective shadows

Various problems can develop when using shadow effects. Here are points to look out for:

- *Stability* can be essential for many subjects. While movement enhances some shadow patterns (e.g., natural foliage), others must be held quite still (e.g., window patterns). Suspended objects and slung projectors can sway!
- *Dilution* from spill-light can gray-out shadows, softening them and reducing their prominence.
- *Sharpness* of cast shadows, is greatest when you use a small point source, with the subject some distance from the light, and relatively close to the background. Avoid stray light diluting the shadow. The background should be flat, and at right angles to the light beam and the subject. Otherwise parts of the shadow will be unsharp. When a shadow is *optically projected*, its sharpness also depends on the quality of the fixture's lens system.
- *Size* of the cast shadow depends on that of the shadowing object, and its relative distance from the lamp and the background. Shadow size grows as the subject moves closer to the lamp, and further from the background. However, these conditions also reduce shadow sharpness, so you may have to compromise here. For *projected shadows*, size depends on the fixture's lens angle, the gobo pattern size, and unit's distance from the background.
- *Distortion* occurs unless the light beam is at right angles to the surface, and the subject and surface are parallel. In many situations, distortion is a natural feature of the effect.

Cast shadows
Any opaque object hung in front of a
hard light source will cast a shadow
(e.g. tree branches, windows,
tracery, cookies). Removing the lens
of a fresnel spot, will improve the
shadow's sharpness, but the light
output will fall

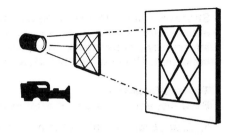

Projected shadows
Stencilled metal *gobos* fitted into
ellipsoidal spotlights, can produce
precise, elaborate light patterns

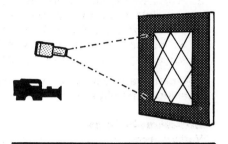

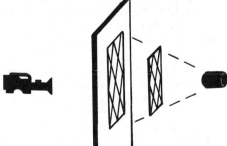

A

Silhouettes
Here emphasis is on the outline of
the subject. You can either place an
unlit subject against a strongly-lit
background as in **A**, or cast (or
rear-project) its shadow onto the
rear of a translucent screen (**B**)

B

91

Controlling shadows

Having keyed the subject with a frontal spotlight so as to provide firm clear-cut modeling, it is very frustrating to find a large distracting shadow spread across the background behind it. Shadowless lighting would reduce modeling and texture. So what is the solution?

Moving the key light

The closer the subject is to the background, the harder it is to avoid casting a shadow onto it.

When the key is *dead frontal* (near the lens), the subject's shadow is immediately behind it, and little or none is visible on camera. As you progressively *offset* the key left or right, the shadow moves out from behind the subject (in the opposite direction). The rate of displacement depends on the subject's distance from the background, so it often helps to move the subject nearer the camera.

Raising the key causes the subject's shadow to fall lower and lower on the background. But remember that at the same time you are emphasizing the subject's modeling (more pronounced nose, neck and eye shadows).

Disguising the shadow

Sometimes you can throw a subject's shadow onto a dark or broken-up part of the background so that it is less prominent. It may even be overlooked altogether. (A boom microphone's shadow, for instance, can remain undetected amongst shadows of foliage.) But if you are not careful you will find that you are degrading the subject's lighting simply in order to subdue the background shadow! When the subject is actually touching the background its shadow will just spread beside it and no amount of re-angling of the key will improve matters. The minimum shadow comes from a key at right angles to the background.

Very occasionally, you can reduce an offending background shadow by closely barndooring the subject's lighting. But as the shadow is cast by the subject itself any light restriction must now leave part of the subject unlit!

'Lighting-out' shadows

It is always tempting to try to eliminate shadows by diluting them with additional light – 'lighting them out'. But this technique has its limitations. By the time you have illuminated the shadow sufficiently to make it unobtrusive, there is a good chance that you will have overlit the background, or created a hotspot there.

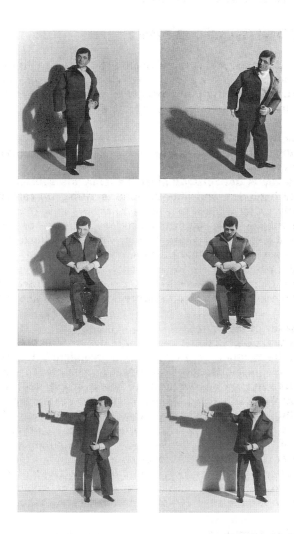

CONTROLLING SHADOWS

Altering the subject-to-background distance
As the subject is moved further from the background, its shadow moves
downwards, and is less distracting

Raising the key light
As you raise the key light, the subject's shadow moves down the background
— and subject modeling is emphasized

Moving the key sideways
As you move the key sideways relative to the camera's position, the subject's
shadow moves in the opposite direction, often becoming elongated

Shadowless lighting

Flood the scene with diffuse light and you cannot avoid uninterestingly flat results. Apply soft light skillfully and the delicate, half-tones it produces can create beautiful effects.

Positioning the soft light
Completely shadowless lighting is normally only used to isolate an object in space. More often a faint shadow or shading is desirable to enhance the illusion of form and space.

The secret is to angle the soft light, confining it to one major direction. Although texture and surface contours can disappear entirely if a soft light source is placed beside the lens, move the lamp to, say, 4H or 8H and 3V–2V, and subtle modeling will develop.

Random light scatter and reflected light usually provide sufficient filler. But where you want to avoid shading and shadow altogether add a low-intensity fill light.

When to use 'shadowless' lighting
Shadowless lighting creates an air of isolation and detachment. The effect is unreal, ethereal. There is a suggestion of weightlessness, purity, a lack of emphasis. On a more down-to-earth level, high key shadowless surroundings are invaluable when shooting highly reflective subjects, such as silver, glass, chromium, and shiny surfaces (plastic, cars).

General light levels should normally be kept quite high when using shadowless illumination. Low intensity soft light is liable to produce a dull 'overcast daylight' effect, which lacks vitality and visual appeal.

A particularly effective approach in which shadows are kept to the minimum, uses soft frontal lighting accompanied by a single hard back light. The subjects are rimmed in a *contre jour* treatment. When carefully controlled, the results can be most attractive and are particularly suitable for classical ballet.

Even background lighting
On the face of it, the simplest way to evenly illuminate a large plain background, is to suspend a series of soft light fixtures. However, unless you are using specially designed *cyc units* (which have a graded light-spread), you may find the spill from adjacent soft light sources overlaps to form random bright patches that are not readily eliminated. (Fresnel spotlights may be preferable, as barndoors can be closed to restrict overlapping light beams, and so avoid 'doubling'.)

Large banks of soft light produce a considerable quantity of heat, compared with more efficient spotlight sources.

Soft key light

If the soft key light is close to the camera, modeling is minimal. Offset the soft key, and we have finely graded shading, and delicate half-tones. Add a hard back light, and the subject is attractively rimmed with light. Its thickness and depth are more apparent

Shadowless lighting

By special arrangements, it is possible to eliminate background shadows altogether

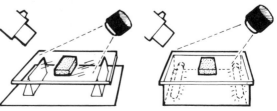

Scenic lighting – the approach

When a set is well designed and carefully lit, the results look so obviously *right*. The pictures have a strong visual appeal. The atmosphere is completely convicing. But the mechanics and techniques that underly the effect are hidden and self-effacing.

General background lighting

In such programs as games shows or talk shows, you are concerned with *general effect*. You are not trying to recreate a particular environment. The setting for this kind of production will usually consist of a large background area (e.g., a cyc) and a series of decorated scenic flats, drapes, screens, etc. which are lit individually with spotlights (shaded or patterned).

Light the background separately from the action wherever possible. Don't rely on random spill from fill light to illuminate it! A background flooded with soft light has little 'character'. And in any case, your fill light should not be bright enough to appreciably lift the background!

Specific background lighting

Whether you are lighting a studio setting or an actual room on location, always begin with a clear idea of the overall effect you are aiming at.

The most flexible approach is to use a series of closely coordinated lamps, each covering a localized area: the doorway, the fireplace, a bookcase, a wall picture . . . and so on. You can then adjust and balance each source, to develop a particular atmospheric effect. The more generalized the background lighting, the less dynamic the pictorial impact is likely to be.

There will be times when you have insufficient equipment, or too little space to light so specifically. Then you may have to compromise and use a single lamp to cover a much larger area of the background. Similarly, you might have to rely on a person's key lighting their background instead of treating them separately.

'Natural lighting'

Very occasionally, you can substitute a single lighting fixture for a natural source and rely on that to fully light the entire scene – e.g., sunlight through the window, or a central ceiling light. But this will seldom suit varying camera viewpoints. Instead, you will usually need to light the background in sections, to simulate the overall *effect* of that source; e.g., light patches on walls, a window shadow, etc.

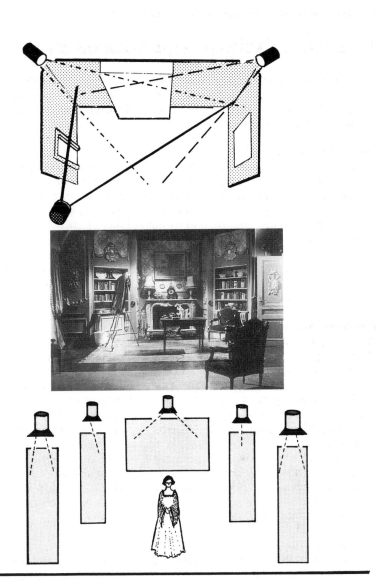

SCENIC LIGHTING

Dual-function lighting
Where settings are small, or facilities limited, you may use action lighting to illuminate the background.

F = Frontal key and back wall
B = Back lights and side walls

Specific background lighting
You can light the background with a series of merged spotlit areas

Alternatively, you can light each section of the scenery with a separate spotlight

Scenic lighting – neutral settings

A *neutral* setting is one that has no environmental associations. A wide variety of productions use neutral backgrounds, including interviews, newscasts, demonstrations, music, dance. The scenery itself is often quite plain and sparse, relying on *lighting* to give it an interesting ambience.

Plain backgrounds

Back-drops (backcloths) or runs of scenic flats are often used to provide plain backgrounds. But the most widely used all-purpose background found in studios, is the *cyclorama* or *cyc cloth*.

You can alter the effective tone of a mid-gray background simply by adjusting its lighting. Strongly lit, it reproduces as white. Leave it unlit, concentrating light on the foreground action area, and it will appear black.

Although mid-gray cycloramas are the most versatile, off-white and blue versions are also used; the latter to represent 'open sky'.

A plain background will look far more attractive if it is gradually shaded; brightest at the bottom, slowly falling off to black above. You can achieve this effect with a *groundrow* of soft lights (troughs, cyc lights, strip lights) resting on the floor. These units will usually need to be hidden behind low scenic pieces (e.g., a *cove, scenic groundrow*).

Alternatively, you can light the background with a row of hung fresnel spotlights, which are barndoored to restrict the light; although this method produces a much sharper cut-off.

Drapes

Drapes in many forms are often used as the basis of neutral settings. If you light them straight-on, their folds (and creases!) are less obvious. The greater the horizontal angle of the light, the more you emphasize their shape; the more sculpted they appear. If you *edge-light* draperies, they tend to lose their softness and flow, and become quite coarsely modeled.

It may require a considerable amount of light to reveal the modeling in darker drape materials (e.g., dark velours). Other materials, that have a shiny, glazed, or light-toned surface, reflect light all too easily, and it may be difficult to avoid hot-spots or over-exposure.

Translucent drapes (sheers, ninons) pose certain problems. When frontally lit, they appear blank and uninteresting, and are easily 'burned-out'. A ¾-back lamp, will reveal their structure. But it is often best to leave them *completely unlit*, and strongly light the background beyond them instead.

98

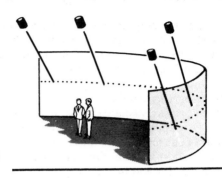

The 'Cyc'
Cycs are widely used as neutral backgrounds. To avoid uneven illumination or varying color quality, make sure that all background lamps are at similar distances from it

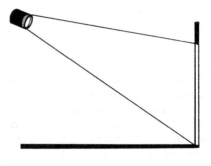

Using fresnel spotlights
You can merge the soft-edged beams of fresnel spots to light the cyc evenly. But they are particularly useful to create shading, blobs, shafts, or patches of light

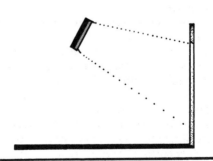

Using soft light
Because soft light falls off rapidly with distance, hung soft light (e.g. scoops) are liable to produce inverted shading, with the top of the cyc over-illuminated, and its base underlit

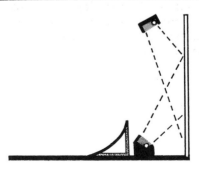

Cyc units
Specially-designed *cyc units* can illuminate the background over a large area from hung and/or floor positions. Hidden behind a ground row, cyc units can provide a graded background, that is lightest at its base

Scenic lighting – decorative effects

You can create endless decorative effects with light; even using simple materials. Shine a spotlight onto a piece of kitchen foil (folded, crushed or bent) to reflect nebulous streaking light patterns across the background. Just a couple of spotlights with different color gels, can create rich variations.

Spotlight patterns

Fresnel spotlights alone can produce a range of light shapes: pointed straight-on to a background they provide light blobs of adjustable size, with graded soft borders. Shining downwards you can form 'arches' of light. At oblique angles, shafts and streaks of light develop. Using barndoors, you can shape their beams into slits, columns, squares and rectangular shapes.

Make holes in a sheet of foil, and place it in front of a spotlight to produce a wide variety of dapples, streaks – even cloud effects.

Projected patterns

Projection spotlights (*ellipsoidal spots*, *profile spots*) are useful for hard-edged spots and light shafts. Some fixtures have internal masks or irises to adjust the spot's size. (Some have additional irises to alter the intensity.) Moving internal shutter blades you can form four-sided pattern shapes.

Inserting small metal stencil *gobos*, you can project many types of detailed light patterns, singly or intermixed: windows, skylines, foliage night city scenes, abstract designs, decorative motifs, flashing signs, logos .... Superimposed images can build up a multi-color design.

Try making gobos from pieces of foil (vari-sized holes, random slits), wire mesh or stamped-out metal sheet. These can produce fantastic light designs, particularly if slightly defocused. Some fixtures will project images from glass slides (photographic, hand drawn, or scratch-off designs).

For a large image, you need a powerful source some distance away (particularly in well lit surroundings) or several joined images. Wide-angle projector lenses (e.g., 35°) tend to have lower light transmission, so produce dimmer images; but they do not need to be so far away from the background.

Finely perforated gobos (e.g., starry skies) pass very little light, so you may need to keep light off backgrounds, to avoid diluting and degrading the pattern.

Gobos with large delicate patterns may distort or bend in a hot fixture, and partially defocus.

Spotlight patterns
Fresnel spotlights can produce a
series of simple but effective light
shapes that can be used for
background decoration

Image distortion
A light pattern is only undistorted
when the projector is at right angles
to a flat background. When projected
from an angle, the shape becomes
increasingly distorted, and overall
sharpness varies. However, the
effect may be quite natural

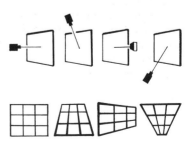

An illusion of reality

If you flood any room with soft light – using a floodlight bank or bounce-light from the ceiling – it will lose any kind of 'atmosphere' and appear quite artificial. On the other hand, if a well-designed studio setting is lit effectively, it will seem totally realistic. Good lighting not only conveys an impression of the physical structure, but it imparts an ambience, conjures a mood.

Creating atmosphere

There are no 'rules' for building an environmental effect. But there are points to guide you, including some reminders of techniques you have already met:

Walls of interiors should usually be shaded (e.g., to shoulder height), but the light cut-off should not be too abrupt. Where there is a single window, that wall will normally be darkest, while the wall opposite will tend to be brightest.

Windows are valuable features in any setting. Light shining in through a window tells us something about the world beyond. While casting decorative patterns onto a wall (or ceiling), it can help to establish the weather, time of day, and sometimes even the location (e.g., water ripple convinces us that this is the cabin of a ship at sea). By adjusting the angle and color of the light, you can suggest sunlight, moonlight, sunset, street lamps, flashing street signs, etc.

Backings are used outside the windows of settings to simulate the exterior scene: anything from plain 'sky' to painted scenic drops or photo-enlargements of street scenes, etc. Even a simple flat decorated with shadows (e.g., a tree branch) can be effective. These are normally lit evenly overall.

Backing are used in interior settings beyond doorways and arches, to prevent cameras *shooting-off* (*over-shooting*) the set, and imply hallways, rooms, etc., beyond. These backings are usually shaded, and may be slightly brighter than the main room, to create an impression of distance.

Ceilings on studio settings not only restrict light access but can themselves be quite difficult to light. Lamps concealed on the ground behind furniture are often the best solution. The ceiling's brightness needs to be adjusted carefully if it is to look convincing.

Practical lamps such as table-lamps or wall-fittings, are usually insufficiently bright to illuminate their surroundings effectively. Instead you will have to 'cheat' the effect, using more powerful lighting fixtures to cast light onto the walls and the performers from appropriate angles.

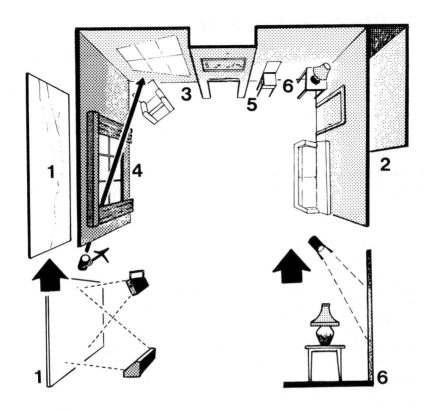

CREATING AN ATMOSPHERE

When lighting a realistic interior scene or an actual room, there are usually several regular features:

1 *Exterior* – Bright scene beyond window creates effect of distance
2 *Interior backing* – Walls outside doorways are usually shaded and slightly brighter than the room, to give an impression of distance
3 *Sunlight* – Hard light through window casts shadows onto a wall
4 *Walls* – Darker window wall helps to emphasize exterior brightness
5 *Room walls* – Walls are normally shaded to about shoulder height, but this will vary to suit any practical wall lights (wall brackets)
6 *Practical lamps* – Their light may not be sufficient to illuminate nearby surfaces. Supplementary spotlights may be needed to simulate the effect

Lighting faults

When preoccupied setting and adjusting lamps, you can easily overlook the odd lighting defects that inevitably occur. Here is a list of regular problems to look out for.

Typical defects and their remedies

Tones. Check the scene for anything that may be too light or dark toned to reproduce well — background tones, furniture, drapes, props, etc. Take care to keep light off over-light areas (leave them unlit; use a barndoor flap or a flag; dim the lamp). For dark areas, increase local lighting as necessary (spot a lamp; add an extra lamp). See that nearby surfaces are not under or over lit as a result. (Aim at a typical maximum contrast range of around 20:1.)

Uneven lighting. Light and shade make a scene look attractive. But take care that exposure does not vary appreciably for different camera positions (e.g., ±½ stop). Check that walls are appropriately and consistently shaded. When flat-lighting surfaces, check through half-closed eyes for any unevenness. (This trick makes irregularities more obvious.)

Distracting highlights. Avoid bright hotspots and strong specular reflections where possible. A coating of dulling (wax) spray on shiny or glossy surfaces makes them less prominent. Sometimes angling or hiding the surface is the answer. You may even need to reposition lamps or the camera.

Unwanted shadows. Stray light may cast accidental shadows of hung lamps, practicals, or scenery onto the background or the performers. It can reveal unevenness in flat backgrounds (sky cloths, cyc, scrims, walls).

Distracting shadows. Even quite natural shadows can draw attention to themselves if they are intrusive, obscure important details, or are distorted.

Multiple shadows. Try to avoid multiple shadows around subjects. Even where this effect is natural enough, it can be very distracting, especially on nearby backgrounds.

Spill light. When you are setting a lamp on a foreground subject, don't forget that its light may reach more distant parts of the scene, and cause unwanted effects there.

Lamps in shot. Take care that your lamps are not going to come into shot. The danger points are: lamps on the set walls seen in long shots or low shots; lamps at the sides of the setting seen in cross shots; lamps outside windows and doors; lamps reflected in mirrors or glass within the setting.

Lens flares. Stray light from back lights can cause lens flares. Lower the top flaps of their barndoors to keep light out of the camera's lens.

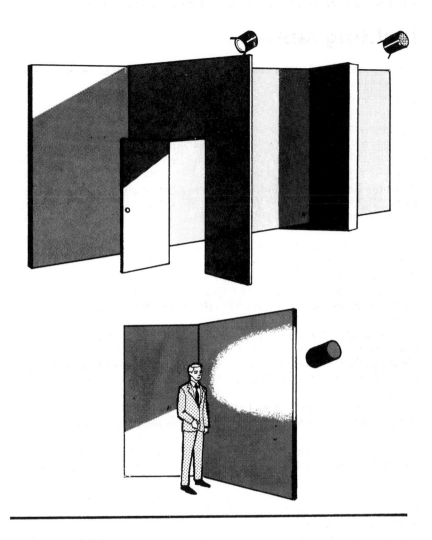

FAULTS IN SCENIC LIGHTING

Structural shadows
On camera, uncontrolled shadows cast by parts of the setting, can give the audience false impressions of shape and distance

Spill light
Take care that action lighting does not accidentally spill onto or 'scrape' nearby walls, and produce distracting, unmotivated highlights

Lighting open areas

You can use several approaches when lighting a large floor area (e.g., over 45 sq m/55 sq yd).

Single lamp coverage
The simplest method is to use a single powerful key light – e.g., a 10 kW tungsten-halogen lamp, or an HMI source. To cover the area effectively, this lamp must usually be at least 4.5 m/15 ft high, and around 6 m/20 ft from the action center. If performers get too close to the key, its vertical angle may prove too steep, and they will be over-lit. If the key is too distant or its vertical angle too shallow, it will be more difficult to avoid shadows (cameras, sound booms, scenery) falling onto the background and the performers.

Dual keys
Here you subdivide the action area into left- and right-hand sections, keeping overlapping lamps to a minimum. Where the action is on either side of the staging area, each half can be keyed separately; both areas sharing common central fill light.

For overall action, you might use *split keys*. Two keys are rigged side-by-side. Vertical barndoors restrict their beams so that each covers half of a 45° spread of light. Similarly, you can use split back lights.

Sectional keys
Another approach is to divide the entire area from front to back, into a series of 4.5 m/15 ft deep 'strips' (diagonally or across the action area). Each section has its own key light, back light, and fill light. There is inevitably an overlap between sections, but if fill light is of fairly high intensity, multiple shadows may not be obtrusive.

Soft frontal
This method uses powerful soft light sources angled either side of the action area, supported by a series of three-quarter back lights. The results can be effective for general action (e.g., dance). However, if there are specific positions where people speak to camera, add a localized hard key, and mark the floor with crayon 'toemarks'.

Localized areas
If the entire area does not need to be lit, you may be able to provide several independent 'pools' or areas, each treated with separate three-point lighting. Occasionally, you can follow action over a large area with one or more follow spots alone.

Opposite keys
When action is split left and right of
the area, a key either side may be
effective. However, it can leave a
central area underlit **(A)** or doubly lit
(B). Supplementary soft light at F
improves the overall coverage

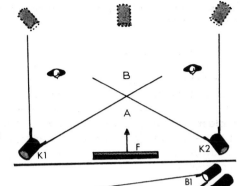

Split keys
Here two adjacent keys combine to
cover a wide angle. Side flaps of
barndoors are adjusted to butt their
beams together

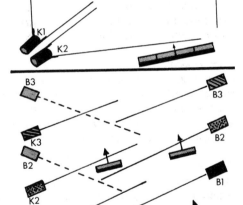

Sectional keys
Each key lights a wedge of the area,
supported by a balancing back light.
Spaced rows of soft lights provide
filler

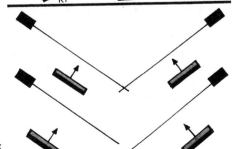

Soft frontal
Where 'soft light' units are powerful
and directional, they may be used to
treat the area in sections; modeling
being provided by a series of ¾-back
lights

107

Lighting in confined spaces

If you place a lamp some distance from the action, it will illuminate a greater area, and its light intensity will remain reasonably constant as people move around. At shorter distances, coverage is more limited, and the light level changes rapidly as the subject distance varies.

Limited space

Both on location and in the studio, you will meet situations where there is barely enough space for the camera, let alone any lighting equipment. Typical problem spots include elevators, tents, closets (cupboards), booths. The trick is to position lamps so that they are not seen on camera, do not get in the way, yet produce an *appropriate* kind of illumination! In some situations, the scene is supposed to be taking place in total darkness!

If visibility is all that matters, then a small hard or soft *camera light* will illuminate the subject, swamping it with light. But *frontal* lighting is seldom appropriate in confined spaces. Not only does it kill any atmosphere, but it will often be reflected as hotspots on the background. If considerably broken up though (with a cookie) the defocused dappled light may be acceptable. However, remember that a camera light will move with the camera, and might over-light close subjects.

Sometimes you can rig a lamp *above* the camera, or direct a spotlight *past* the camera, barndooring it tightly to avoid camera shadows. You may be able to attach small lamps to nearby structures (screwed, clipped, taped, or clamped) either side of the action, and use barndoor shutters to avoid light streaks on the background. Lamps on lighting stands often get in the way, and are too easily knocked. Top lighting may be justified (as in an elevator) but can produce very unattractive facial modeling. Overall illumination from bounce light reflected from the ceiling usually destroys any sense of confined space in the picture.

Restricted access

A camera can poke its lens through a hole in the wall, but can you light what it sees on the other side? In a setting you may be able to light the subject through a gap left between two flats through an open door or a window. It may be possible to place a lighting fixture out of shot behind furniture, or conceal it behind a soffit or buttress.

Safety is essential in confined spaces, where hot lamps can fall or overbalance, and scorch or set fire to nearby surfaces. Conceal or suspend all cables to prevent accidents.

108

CONFINED SPACES

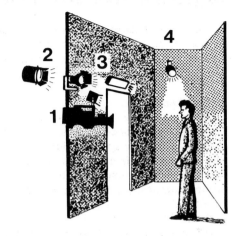

Restricted space
Under cramped conditions, lamps can be:

1 Fixed to the camera
2 Directed over the camera
3 Hung or attached over the camera access point
4 Fastened onto side walls, out of the camera's shot

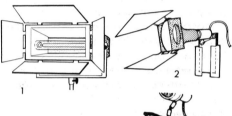

Useful lighting fixtures
Small lightweight units for use in confined spaces include:

1 Small broad (nook-light)
2 Internal reflector lamp (PAR lamp) attached to a wall (or pipe) with a profiled plate
3 Hand-held lamp (which may also be supported in a screw gaffer grip)
4 Sprung alligator clip (clipped to flat or furniture)
5 Lensless spotlight on lightweight stand

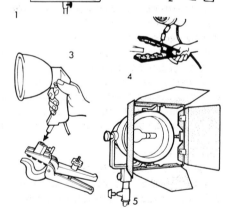

Restricted access
When regular lamps cannot reach the action, fixtures may be concealed:

1 Behind architectural features
2 Behind furniture
3 On the floor

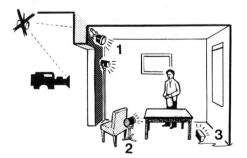

Lighting translucent backgrounds

Translucent backgrounds are constructed from stretched sheets of cloth or plastic. They can be used in a number of ways: as screens for rear projection, to display patterns and decorative effects, as opaque panels, to provide backings to decorative screens, etc.

Methods of lighting

Lit from the front, a translucent surface will look like a plain flat undecorated surface. It is only when you light it from behind, and reduce frontal lighting that its particular magic appears.

If you do the obvious and rear-light a translucent background with a single lamp on the ground or a lighting stand the camera will see a pronounced hot-spot that changes position as it moves around. The size of the bright area will depend on the area and distance of the lighting fixture.

You can rear-light the screen more evenly, by using either a distant spotlight hung above the screen height, or two lamps cross-lighting at about 45°.

A row of strip lights on the ground behind the screen (ground row, cyc lights), will produce a gradated effect – lighter at the bottom, falling away in intensity towards the top. If the lamps are too close to the screen, there is a danger that the base of the screen may appear too bright on camera.

Shadow effects

The simplest way to create a silhouette is to place an unlit subject in front of a rear-lit screen.

Alternatively, you can cast shadows and patterns onto the translucent screen (front or back) by any of the methods we discussed earlier: gobos in projectors, cast shadows, etc. By cross-fading between lamps you can mix patterns, or transform from one to another with ease.

You can produce very successful shadows and silhouettes by placing subjects such as furniture, netting, cut-out stencils, foliage, close to the back of the screen, and rear-lighting them with a compact hard light source.

Using two (or more) light sources, you can create *multiple decorative shadows* in different shades or colors. The light from one lamp will tend to dilute the shadow from another, producing tonal and color mixtures.

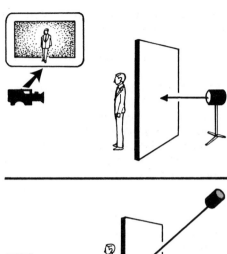

Central lighting
Central rear lighting produces a
central bright area, falling off in
intensity at the edges

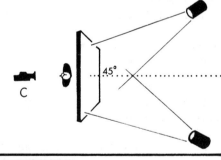

Even lighting
You can light the background
evenly, with either a single distant
hung lamp, or two sources either
side angled at 45°

Graded background
A groundrow can provide
attractively graded background
lighting

111

Lighting multi-level staging

Most action in the studio takes place at floor level. But there are situations where raised areas are needed and these bring their own particular problems.

Platforms/parallels/rostra

Demountable platforms of various heights are used in scenic design. They range from a slight step-up of a few centimeters to raised areas a couple of meters or so high (e.g., over 6 ft). As well as simulating architectural features, these *platforms* (also called *parallels*, *rostra*, *risers*) are used to provide interesting layouts or displays and to give more varied camera shots for choirs, bands, orchestras, fashion shows, audiences, etc. Multi-level treatments are built up by joining platforms of different heights.

You may be able to use the same key light to illuminate both the people at ground level and those on the platforms. However, if the platforms are high, you will need a powerful lamp some distance away to cover the entire area. Then performers' shadows are likely to fall onto the background. This may not matter. But if, for example, the background is a scenic cloth or a sky-cyc, shadows would ruin the illusion. You can raise the communal key in order to lower shadows, but this is liable to degrade portraiture for people at floor level.

In these circumstances, it is better to arrange two sets of key lights instead: one for the lower action, and the other for performers on the raised areas.

Back light, too, requires care. People on the platforms are closer to hung lamps than those at ground level, so their back light may prove to be too intense.

Stairs

If one lamp alone is used to cover an entire staircase, the lighting angle may become too steep towards the foot of the stairs. Instead, it may be better to use two (or more) localized keys to cover it.

Backlight is best arranged straight down the stairs. Its barndoor is side-shuttered, to prevent light streaking down the wall; edge-lighting it, revealing irregularities, and casting long shadows. A top barndoor flap prevents lens flares on a camera looking up the stairs. You can also side light action, preferably barndooring the lamp to a diagonal slit which follows the line of the stairs. But keep this light well confined to enhance an impression of enclosure.

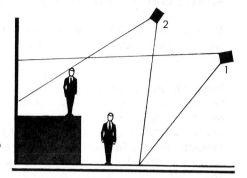

Single-key coverage

1 If a common key is at a suitable height for people at ground level, it may be too shallow for those on the platform
2 If the key is raised to overcome this problem, it becomes too steep for ground level action

Separate key lights

Action at floor and platform levels may be lit separately. But look out for:

1 Distracting background shadows
2 The back light for floor action overlighting those on the platform

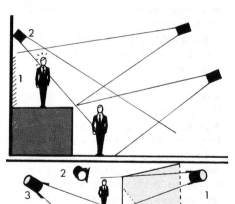

Stairs

1 This long staircase has been subdivided with three localized key lights
2 The back light is shuttered against lens flares and wall streaks
3 The side light follows the line of the stairs

113

Using a follow spot

The *follow* or *following spotlight* is a familiar adjunct to stage presentations, and large area spectacles. It is a device to draw the audience's attention to a selected subject; by itself, or within a group. It isolates with light. You can use it as the *sole illumination*, leaving the surroundings in darkness, or to provide a *pool of light* within a lit scene.

Design

The true *follow* spot is specially designed to follow action smoothly and accurately. It is essential if you want to follow rapid or intricate movement – e.g., fast dance sequences, skaters, acrobats etc. Where there is little or no movement, you can improvise by using a projection spotlight (ellipsoidal spot, profile spotlight, effects projector). At a pinch, you can even use a fresnel spotlight with a cylindrical snoot attached.

The light source of a typical follow spotlight may be tungsten-halogen (e.g., 3 kW), or a metal-halide source (HMI, CSI).

Despite its bulk, the unit is balanced to enable it to be swung around rapidly and easily, with precision. It has various in-built controls for adjusting the area of the spotlight beam, altering its edge sharpness, and varying beam brightness. There may also be color filters and masks to shape the beam (e.g., star outline).

Operating the follow spot

As the performer moves around, the spot operator keeps the disc of light centered. As the action changes, he may broaden the beam to include widespread arm movements, or restrict it to illuminate just one hand.

You have probably seen follow spotlights in use many times. But do not underestimate the operational skills needed. The follow spot is usually a long way from the subject (e.g., a 'throw' of 12–18 m/40–60 ft) in order to have a clear coverage of the action. Even slight movements of the spotlight are magnified considerably at this distance. So the operator requires fine judgement and a steady hand, to continuously locate the light beam accurately. Nothing looks cruder than a shot in which the spotlight misses the subject, or is offset and lights only part of it, or fails to keep up with movement!

When a spotlight has to be lit on cue, and hit its subject immediately (no nervous searching or repositioning when he discovers it is off target!), this is done either by sighting, or by pre-checking the spot position surreptitiously beforehand, while audience attention is elsewhere, using a small dimmed beam.

114

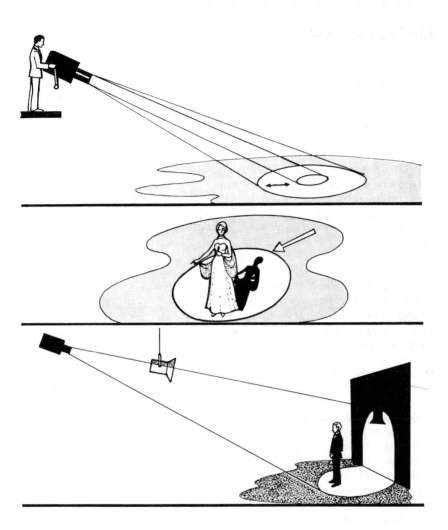

USING THE FOLLOW SPOTLIGHT

Spotlight coverage
The area of the pool of light is adjustable to suit the subject. Maximum
coverage depends on its lens system, and distance from the subject (throw)

Positioning the post
Check the position of the subject's shadow within the disc of light on the
floor. If there is little space between shadow and spot edge, even slight
movements are liable to leave part of the subject unlit

Obstructions
Check that no hung scenery or lamps come within the follow spot's field of
action, and cast shadows

115

On location – interiors

The various techniques we have been looking at, can be used as effectively on location as in the studio. But location lighting usually involves more improvisation and compromise. Lighting complexity varies considerably between productions. Some rely on a quick impromptu setup; others give an opportunity to install a full lighting rig. Anticipation and adaptability are essential, when shooting on location!

The project
When the interior is spacious, and you have only a few lighting fixtures, your options are limited. The best solution is to restrict how much the camera can see. Use *close shots*. Use a window, door or arch to cut off part of the distant scene. Sometimes you can *mask-off* the action area with lightweight screens. Perhaps you can light just a small section of the interior, shoot the action there, and then go on to light the next adjoining section. Edited together, action can look continuous.

The beam angle of most *fresnel* spotlights is too narrow to allow the light to spread sufficiently in small interiors. So broader-beam sources are preferable.

Generally speaking, where space is very limited, softer light of lower intensity is most useful. A small spotlight in an umbrella reflector may suffice in very cramped surroundings. *Lensless spotlights* (*red-heads*) are very versatile. *Small broads* provide overall hard or soft light. In large interiors, *flood-light banks* (*mini-brutes*) offer wide-angle diffuse illumination.

When action is widespread or unpredictable, it may be necessary to illuminate an interior by reflecting light from the ceiling or a wall. The overall diffuse *bounce light* is characterless, inefficient, and often of poor color quality, especially when reflected from colored surfaces. Nearby mirrors, glass and metalwork can reflect mysterious streaks and light patches over the scene!

Prevailing conditions
Just occasionally, you meet situations where the prevailing lighting conditions are ideal. You can position your subject to suit the existing lighting. Perhaps by adding reflected light, or an odd lamp, you can compensate for any shortcomings. Replacing the bulbs in the location lighting fittings with high-intensity versions (e.g., photofloods) could help. But for many situations, it may be better to disregard the existing illumination, and provide your own lighting treatment instead.

116

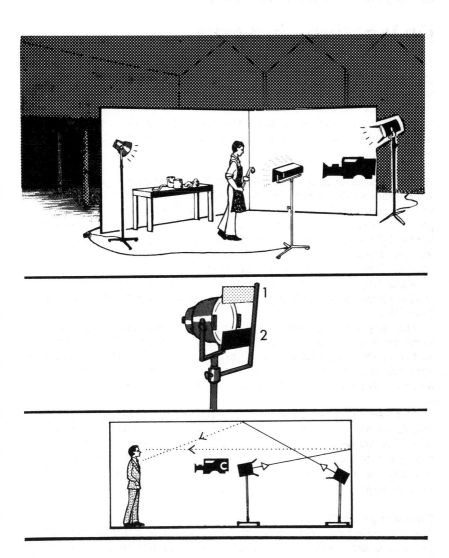

LOCATION INTERIORS

Restricting coverage
If the area seen by the camera is deliberately restricted (e.g. by canvas screens), the action can be lit more economically

Controlling light
You can spread the light from a single lamp across the scene, then use scrim/diffuser (1) and/or a flag (2) to locally control its intensity and coverage

Bounce light
To provide soft overall filler, you can reflect light from the ceiling or walls (or reflectors)

117

On location – exteriors

When shooting in daylight, you really have three choices: accept whatever light conditions you get, until conditions improve, or supplement the natural light.

Natural light
Daylight is continually altering. The light's quality (hardness/diffusion) and tonal contrast, its intensity, and its color quality can vary from minute to minute. The sun's direction and vertical angle (azimuth) change throughout the day.

Although you can alter exposure (automatically perhaps) to compensate for differing light levels, and re-adjust the camera's white balance, you can do little about changes in light quality and direction. Sunlight creates strong modeling and relatively high contrasts. Its *vertical angle* is often too steep for attractive portraiture (40°–90°), and its direction changes throughout the day, from east to west (via south).

Most scenes appear flat and least attractive under overcast skies. Sun from behind the camera can model effectively, but subjects lack depth at lower angles. From either side, the modeling is dynamic and somewhat harsh. Shooting with the sun shining towards the camera as a back light can produce extremely attractive effects; although planes facing the camera may be underlit. Check for lens flares; not always obvious in a camera's small viewfinder.

Compensatory lighting
When skies are cloudy, a strong key light near the camera can considerably improve the subject's modeling. But under brighter conditions even powerful arc lights appear puny. Where the sun is in the wrong direction the best solution may be to reposition the camera and action so that sunlight is from the side or rear and use reflected light or lamps to illuminate areas in the shade. If the sunlight is much too bright and contrasty a large sheet of scrim held over the subject may improve matters.

Reflectors are simply large boards held up to reflect sunlight onto the subject. The reflected light quality depends on the surface you use: from metal foil (hard) to matte white (soft). The greater the coverage you need, the larger the reflector must be. Reflectors are very susceptible to wind rock. Most important, they always depend on the sun shining, from an appropriate direction!

Portable lighting units using nickel cadmium batteries can be useful on close exterior shots (as key or filler); but for higher powered lamps, public supplies or power lines from portable generators become necessary.

118

EXTERIORS

Natural light
Natural light can prove quite unsatisfactory. Here important details are in deep shadow, and the lighting contrast is excessive

Reflectors
You can use reflector boards to reflect sunlight, to provide key light or fill light. How effectively depends on the board's surface finish, and the prevailing light conditions

119

Scenic insertion

There are various methods of inserting a picture from a slide or another video source into a camera's shot: to provide a display panel or a background scene.

Scenic projection

Rear projection (*back projection*; *BP*) was once used to provide complete backgrounds behind action, but is now mainly found in *wall display screens*, and for small window backings. An image of the scene is projected onto the rear of a translucent screen, while the camera shoots action from the reverse side.

The main problem is in avoiding light falling onto the screen, casting shadows and washing out the image. To shield light off the screen, subjects need to be at least 2 m/6½ ft away.

In *reflex projection*, the background picture from a slide is front projected onto a special glass-beaded screen. Its size can vary from a small display screen to a total background. The slide image is projected onto the screen via an angled 'see-through, mirror' positioned in front of the camera lens. (Accurate set-up is critical.) The camera sees anyone standing in front of the screen, as if located in the background scene. Because the highly-efficient screen only reflects light back over a very narrow angle, little of the spill light is reflected. The projected scene is not visible on the brightly lit performers, and their own shadows are hidden behind them.

Scenic insertion

There are two methods of electronically inserting into a video camera's shot. In *keyed insertion* (*luminance keying*; *inlay*) a selected area of the main shot is 'cut out', and replaced by an identical area of another source (camera, film, VTR, slide scanner). Any foreground action moving into this part of the shot is cut off. However, there are no restrictions for lighting.

Chroma key (*CSO*) is a more widely used, sophisticated system. Here a person stands in front of a blue backdrop (other hues can be used). Wherever the video-switching circuits see blue in the master shot, they switch to another video source, which is showing the background scene. The result is a composite picture with the subject integrated into the background.

The blue backdrop has to be reasonably evenly lit for shadows or patches can cause false switching. If the foreground scene includes (or reflects) any blue, there will be spurious breakthrough or edge-ragging. To create the illusion that the foreground subject is *within* a background picture the lighting, contrast, tonal and color quality etc., must match quite closely.

120

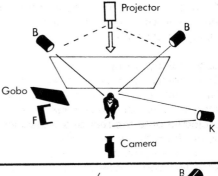

Rear projection (back projection, BP)
The camera sees the person
standing in front of a scene
projected onto a screen. Foreground
spill light must be kept to a
minimum

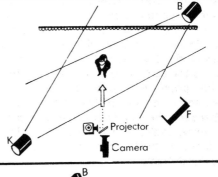

Reflex projection
The camera sees both the subject,
and the bright reflected image on the
front-projected scene. Little of the
foreground lighting falling onto the
screen is reflected towards the
camera

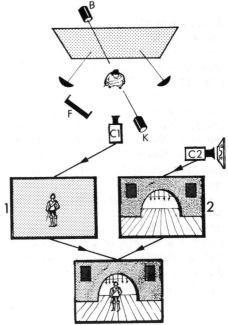

**Chroma key (color separation
overlay, CSO)**
The subject is placed in front of a
blue background. Wherever circuitry
detects blue in the subject's
camera's picture (**Cam 1**), it switches
to another video source (**Cam 2**). The
composite shot combines subject
and background

121

Lighting changes

One of the most intriguing features of light, is the way you can completely change a scene's appearance at the touch of a button. The basic mechanics are simple enough: individual lamps or groups of lamps are switched, or faded to different intensities. But the kinds of changes you make will really depend on your facilities. The skill lies in the subtlety and effectiveness of these changes; how smoothly you introduce them.

Making the lighting change
There are several situations where you will need to make a lighting change:

- *Load reduction*; to reduce heat, avoid stray light, and save power, it is good practice to switch off all lighting fixtures in settings you are not actually shooting.
- A *preparatory change*; e.g., transforming a setting from day to night, ready for the next action there. Even where your control facilities are very limited, you can switch or plug-up/unplug lamps, to make major changes between scenes.
- *Developments during a scene*; e.g., day breaks, and the room gradually begins to grow lighter. This may involve anything from simply switching or fading one lamp, to elaborate variations in which some lamps grow brighter while others are dimmed, all to different intensities!
- *Action cue*; e.g. Someone switches off a bedside lamp. Anything from simple switching, to cross-switching, in which a new set of lamps comes on ('moonlight' perhaps), as the main lighting is extinguished. Because the lighting change has to coincide with action, this can be 'cheated' by the actor just putting a hand on the light switch, while you operate the control board. Alternatively, you may have relay circuits that enable the practical lamp's switch to control the lighting change.

Pictorial changes
Lighting changes can be used in several ways to enhance the presentation of a program:

Presentation: Here a lighting change is used to introduce and/or close a show. For example, the guest is announced, and a spotlight stabs the darkness to reveal her. The lights on speakers are faded to silhouette them against a lit background.

Decorative changes: A song ends, and the cyc patterns and colors change. Rhythmical switching emphasizes the musical beat.

Environmental changes: Atmospheric lighting alters to suit the action or the mood. Someone enters a room and switches on lights.

Temporal changes: In a drama, the room darkens as night falls.

Background patterns
Just by changing the patterns
projected onto the background, you
can completely alter the picture's
impact. The size, shape, and tone of
the background patterns can affect
the subject's prominence, its
strength, its significance

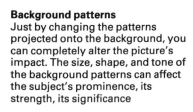

Using colored light

Because the video camera provides color pictures, one might assume that colored light would play a major part in lighting techniques. In most productions it is used for limited background or decorative treatment. Color offers many traps for the unwary!

Color medium

You can produce coloured light in a wide range of hues and intensities by placing sheets of dyed plastic or gelatin over lighting fixtures. While plastic sheets are more costly, they are non-inflammable and waterproof, remarkably durable, and keep their color. Gelatine sheeting is quite cheap but it is brittle, distorts and discolors in use.

Do not fasten color medium directly over a lighting fixture, but fit it into a suitable metal 'color-frame' which clips over the front of the fixture, and allows air to circulate freely. This avoids over-heating and so prolongs the useful life of both the medium and the lamp bulb.

Don't try to judge any color medium by holding it up to the light. Instead, shine light through it, because a lamp's brightness and color temperature, and the surface's color/texture all influence the final effect. Never underestimate the effect of color temperature. A white surface lit by 'white' light from a series of lamps working at different color temperatures, can appear to be multi-hued – orange, yellow, blue.

Colored light on people

Unless you want startling effects, think twice before lighting people with colored light. You can use subtle shades of yellow-orange for certain effects such as candlelight or firelight, or light blue for moonlight, but the effect soon palls. Generally speaking, only white light produces really attractive portraiture. Even uncorrected low or high color temperature lighting, gives an artificial, unreal quality to skin tones; and faces can appear sallow, ill, flushed, or grubby.

Colored light on backgrounds

There are really two applications for colored light. The first is to create *naturalistic effects*; as when you light a cyclorama to resemble a blue sky, or a sunset. The second is to develop *decorative effects* that suit the ambience of the program, the mood of the occasion.

Strong background colors can affect the way faces appear on the screen! Subjectively, skin tones seem to move towards a complementary hue. Warm background colors make faces appear cooler (bluish). Cool colors will warm the skin tones.

USING COLORED LIGHT

Light mixtures – additive primaries
Light of different hues will combine
to form new color mixtures. Here
beams of red, blue and green light
blend to produce new secondary
colors: magenta (purple), cyan
(blue-green), and yellow

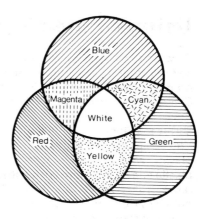

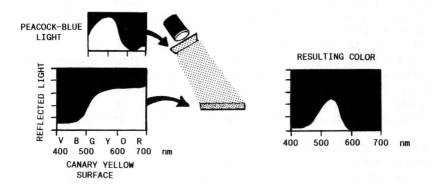

Colored surfaces
Where colored light falls onto a surface of a different hue, the result depends
on their relative spectral coverage

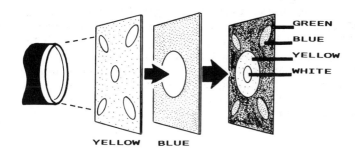

Multi-color effects
Sandwiches of cut-out color medium can produce multi-color effects

Lighting graphics

A wide variety of *graphics* (*captions*) are used in video production, including photographs, charts, maps, plans, artwork, title-cards, etc.

Although many graphics are now produced electronically (using character generators and video effects), there are still situations where it is easiest to present them directly in front of a camera. A speaker can point to features. The camera can move around selectively picking out particular details.

Problems
Normally, shooting graphics presents no appreciable lighting problems except:

- *Shading* – The surface appears brighter at the top, or to one side. This may be due to the lighting all coming from an oblique angle. Alternatively it can be caused by the surface not being flat on to the lens (i.e., warped, or angled).
- *Hot-spots* – A very bright circular area can obscure detail, if the surface is shiny/glossy, or the lamp used has uneven coverage ('spotty', central hot-spot). If the graphic is behind galss or clear plastic (e.g. a framed picture), there is always the danger of flares or specular reflections. Slight angling is the usual cure.
- *Exaggerated texture or unevenness* – Where graphics are wrinkled or buckled, have dents or blemishes, or are made from materials with varying surface finishes, extra care is necessary. Angled lighting (edge-light) will certainly exaggerate any of these features.
- *Shadows* – Usually found in multi-layer graphics, where one layer can shadow the next beneath it.

The solutions
To illuminate a flat surface perfectly evenly, it is best to light it from both left and right edges (or from top to bottom) with diffused light sources. Failing that, use a fresnel spotlight some 3 m/10 ft or so away, at a vertical angle of about 20° to 30°.

Pepper's ghost
Anything lit along the center line of the lens (the 'lens axis') will appear absolutely shadowless. You can achieve this effect by placing a sheet of clean clear glass at 45° in front of the camera lens. A spotlight pointed at the glass, is reflected straight onto the subject. Although much of the light is wasted, the method is very effective, and can be used to light multi-layered graphics, where flaps, or pull-out sections, etc., could cast shadows.

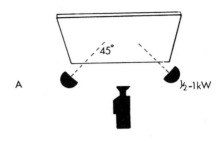

A

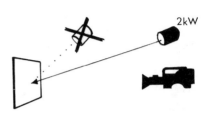

B

Lighting set-up

A For even lighting, a soft source either side of the graphic is ideal

B It is often necessary to use a hung spotlight (to keep the floor clear of lighting stands). Avoid steep lighting, for this produces vertical shading

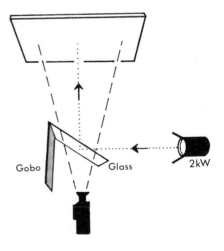

Pepper's ghost

For shadowless even illumination, reflect light from a spotlight, using a glass or clear plastic sheet at 45° to the camera lens axis. (The gobo prevents light spilling beyond)

Gobo   Glass

The lighting plot

There are really two ways of beginning the lighting process.

The sketch plot
Here you stand beside the subject (or where it will be), and systematically consider the direction and position of each lighting fixture.

While doing this, you draw a *sketch plot* of your decisions, with major 'landmarks' to indicate where lamps are to be located. Lines from the lamp symbols to chairs, doorways, etc., show their purpose. A number beside each symbol shows the power outlet that is to feed it (*patching*). Whether you then rig and set each lamp in turn, or wait until you have finished assessing the overall treatment, is your choice.

The prepared plot
In the second method, you work out your entire lighting strategy *beforehand* on a scale plan of the studio. This shows the outlines of settings, overhead battens (barrels), grid, etc.

Different symbols identify the various *types* of lighting fixture needed, together with detailed information on *accessories* (color medium, flags, diffusers), *lamp supports* (hangers, clamps, lighting stands), *power* arrangements (plugging/patching, cable routing). Again, lines show each lamp's direction and coverage.

This comprehensive *lighting plot* is then used to rig and plug all the fixtures, and guide the subsequent lamp setting.

The plot's purpose
A plot can serve several purposes. It helps to rationalize your thoughts on how you are going to tackle a project. It is a guide to the amount of equipment needed. (Better to discover at this stage that you do not have enough lamps, than while rigging the show!) It is an aid to estimating the work effort and time required. Because the plot shows each lamp's purpose, one can anticipate potential problems when *rigging* the fixtures.

Where a setting is left in place for regular use (*permanent set*) or to be re-set later, the plot serves as a continuous reference, helping you to achieve consistent results.

What plots do not show
A plot is a valuable guide and a record to major *mechanics*. It can't indicate the *effects* of the lighting. It does not normally show lamp heights, vertical angles and coverage. Fader settings may sometimes be included on the patching sheet.

LIGHTING PLOTS

Lamp stencil
Stencil with symbols for different
forms of lighting fixtures

Left column: Fresnel spotlight,
lensless reflector spot, HMI arc
Center column: Scoop, Softlight
(internally reflected), small broad
Right column: Cyc/light/ground
row, effects spot/profile spot, follow spot

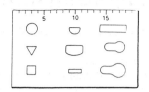

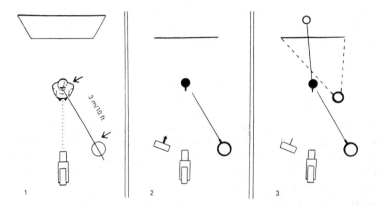

Drawing the plot
1 Consider the key light direction; offset from the nose line.
2 Draw a symbol for the person, and a key light symbol, a minimum of
   3 m/10 ft away. Add fill light on the opposite side to the key
3 Add a slightly offset back light
4 Light the background systematically, to suit the production (realistic,
   decorative, neutral)
5 Allocate power supply channels to the lamps and write channel numbers
   in or beside the symbols

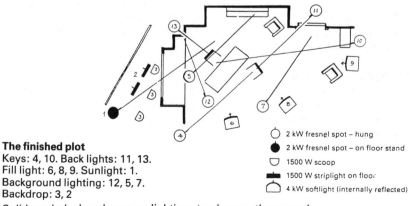

The finished plot
Keys: 4, 10. Back lights: 11, 13.
Fill light: 6, 8, 9. Sunlight: 1.
Background lighting: 12, 5, 7.
Backdrop: 3, 2

○ 2 kW fresnel spot – hung
● 2 kW fresnel spot – on floor stand
▽ 1500 W scoop
▬ 1500 W striplight on floor
⌂ 4 kW softlight (internally reflected)

Solid symbols show lamps on lighting stands or on the ground

129

Setting lamps

Now the lighting fixtures are in position, you need to adjust their coverage and intensities to fit your planned treatment.

Typical approaches
If you have all the lighting fixtures switched on at the same time, glare and overlapping will make judgements very difficult! Instead, switch one fixture on, adjust it, then add the next, until you have built up a completely blended effect. Tackle all protrait/action lighting in a set first – then light backgrounds. Finally set any effects lighting (light patterns).

Adjusting the fixture
Some lighting fixtures are adjusted by hand, others can also be controlled by a hook-on extensible light pole. *Soft light sources* are tilted and turned to cover just the selected area, taking care to avoid over-illuminating backgrounds. *Fresnel spotlights* are fully spotted, pointed at the center of the area to be lit, then flooded to an appropriate coverage and intensity. You can fold barndoor flaps inwards to restrict the light, preventing overlapping beams ('doubling'), undesirable shadows, excess light-spread. With *projectors*, check the evenness of illumination, and then adjust focus for the sharpest image.

Judging the lamp's effect
You can assess lamp adjustments best from the camera's position. But what if a person you are lighting has not yet arrived, and you have no stand-in? There are two main methods:

1. Standing in the subject's marked position with your back to the light, watch your shadow on the floor or background. Guide the person setting the spotlight, by centralizing the fully-spotted lamp on your body. Then flood it and check its coverage.
2. From the subject's position, use a *dark viewing filter*, and look into the flooded spotlight. Have it tilted/turned so that the bright filament image appears located in the center of the fresnel lens. Then it will be centered on you. (You can guide barndoor adjustments similarly.) *Never look directly at a lamp without using a filter*! It produces strong after-images and impairs your visual judgement, preventing your assessing tonal values accurately.

Checking coverage
To check each lamp's coverage when setting it, or tracing hot-spots or shadows, wave a hand or light pole over it while watching the moving shadow. Hold out a hand and trace its shadow(s). Switching the lamp off/on (*flashing*) can help, too.

130

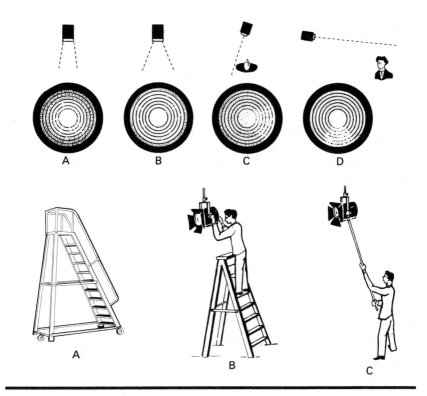

A   B   C   D

A   B   C

SETTING LAMPS

Setting a fresnel spotlight
Looking through a viewing filter from the subject position, the light pattern in the lens shows that the lamp is:

(a) Fully spotted
(b) Fully flooded
(c) Turned slightly to the left
(d) Tilted upwards

Adjusting hung lamps
Regular methods of adjusting hung lighting fixtures, include:

(a) Wheeled lighting ladder
(b) Portable steps, and
(c) A lighting pole

Each has its advantages and limitations

Identifying lamps
To identify which lamp(s) is lighting a surface (or casting shadows), hold out a finger, and extend a line from the shadow to your finger, onwards to the lamp. Here as well as the key (1), there is spill light from another lamp (2)

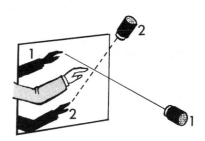

Rehearsals

After preliminary planning, many directors wait until they are actually seeing pictures before finalizing shots. So camera rehearsals, however brief, form an essential part of the lighting process, for then you can update, check and correct treatment.

Initial lighting

You design the lighting with particular subject and camera positions in mind. If these are changed, the lighting may no longer be appropriate. You then have to decide how you are going to alter the treatment to compensate; e.g., whether it is best to re-angle the present key, rig a new one, or re-balance existing lamps to suit the revised shot.

Checking pictures

Within the production control room, there are a number of *picture monitors*. Most are *preview monitors*: each showing the continuous output of its associated camera. A central *master monitor* (*line monitor, line out*) displays the studio output as selected by the production *switcher*; the version that is being videotaped or transmitted. By keeping a critical eye on each of these monitors you can quickly detect any lighting defects; such as unwanted shadows, inappropriate lighting balance, unsuitable light directions.

Trouble shooting

Throughout rehearsals, your lighting plot aids rapid lamp identification for you can see at a glance which lamps are lighting the area shown in a camera's shot. Continually assess problems. If you see a hotspot or shadow, check the plot and switch the most likely lamp's channel. Flashing the lamp will cause the fault to come and go. (If it doesn't, you've got the wrong lamp!) Some problems may require the cooperation of other members of the team (designer, cameraman, sound man, etc).

If you have a *lighting control board* you will be able to correct balance errors immediately as they appear. Other shortcomings may be minor and only need slight barndoor adjustments. But before making major alterations (e.g., moving a key), check that *earlier shots* (which were quite successful in rehearsal) will not now be affected! You may decide to correct each fault as you see it (this may interrupt your watching rehearsal pictures, and distract performers), or to list alterations for attention during a rehearsal break. If someone is assisting you, they may correct or trouble-shoot, while you evaluate pictures, and concentrate on adjusting lighting balance, cues, etc.

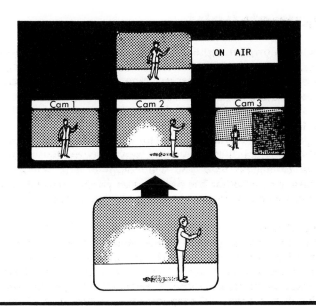

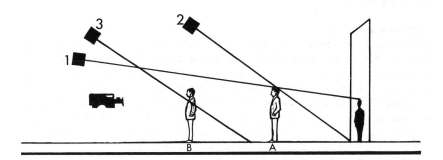

CHECKING THE LIGHTS

Using preview pictures
In a multi-camera production, you can check preview cameras' shots to look out for any lighting faults before they appear 'on-air'. Here a 'hot lamp' on the background, is visible on Cam 2's preview

Anticipate the effect of alterations
If you alter a lamp, will it affect other shots?
Person **A's** background shadow is obtrusive when lit by Key **1**.
Raising the key to **2** reduces (lowers) the shadow. But when he moves forwards to position **B**, he is now out of the light! So an extra key **3** will be needed for this second position

Measuring light

When shooting on *film*, regular checks with a light meter are essential if you are going to avoid accidental over or under exposure; for results are only visible later after processing. The *video* camera has the great advantage that you can assess effects *immediately*, and compensate for any exposure discrepancies, unsuitable contrast, etc., while shooting.

Appropriate light levels

Because the lens aperture is adjusted for correct exposure, we often find on location, that the *f*/stop (and depth of field) largely depends on the prevailing light levels. In the studio, you have direct control of light intensities, so can adjust them to suit a particular lens aperture.

If you light to *high* light levels in the studio you will need more powerful lighting fixtures, which consume considerable power. The heat and glare can make working conditions uncomfortable. If the light levels are greater than the camera needs you will have to reduce them, or stop the lens down to compensate.

Conversely, if you light to *low* light levels, you may need fewer lamps of lower power. But subtle lighting becomes much more difficult for it is harder to assess tonal contrasts accurately in dimmer surroundings. Shading and shadows that appear slight to the eye, may be very prominent on the screen.

Approaches to measurement

Having set up camera equipment to a 'standard' light level (e.g., 1600 lux/150 fc incident at 2900 K) you adjust the lighting to match these parameters.

It is most convenient to measure the *incident light* falling on the scene, and adjust fixtures' outputs to suit (power, focusing, lamp-switching, distance, diffusers, dimmers). Alternatively, you can measure the *surface brightness* of faces, lightest tones, shadows, to assess both light levels and the contrast range. (*Average reflected light* measurements can be misleading, so are less useful.)

As you become familiar with particular equipment, you will soon discover appropriate lamp powers and distances that suit your conditions. For example, a fully flooded 2 kW spotlight some 4 m/13 ft away could provide an appropriate key light intensity. Soft light units might be hung 3 m/10 ft away.

If you are using a *dimmer board* with its faders all set to '7' (49% output), this will allow you to boost or dim fixtures where necessary (moving faders 7–10, or 7–5) yet still keep the *color temperature* within a ±150° Kelvin margin.

CAMERA SENSITIVITY

The effective sensitivity depends on the type of pickup device used (i.e. the kind of camera tube or CCD image sensor fitted), the working lens aperture and electronic adjustment of the video system. Any filter or prompter attachment will cut down the light to the lens.

Taking $f/4$ as a typical working lens aperture, then light levels may be anything from 75–250 foot-candles (lumens per square foot) or 800–2700 lux (lumens per square meter).

The relative amount of light needed at various lens apertures (taking $f/4$ as unity) varies:

$f/1.4$	2	2.8	3.5	4	4.5	5	5.6	6.3	8
⅛	¼	½	¾	1	1¼	1½	2	2½	4

←————— Less light ————— ——— More light ———→

Typical video camera sensitivities

Pickup device	Typical light levels		f-stop
Plumbicon (lead oxide vidicon)			
1¼ in (32 mm)	116–150 fc	1250–1600 lux	* $f/4$
1 in (25 mm)	75 fc	800 lux	* $f/2.8$
⅔ in (18 mm)	56– 70 fc	600– 750 lux	* $f/2$
CCD sensor			
⅔ in (18 mm)	30– 46 fc	325– 500 lux	* $f/2$
½ in (13 mm)	28 fc	300 lux	$f/2$

*These f-stops provide similar depth of field

1 lux = 0.0929 fc   1 fc = 10.764 lux

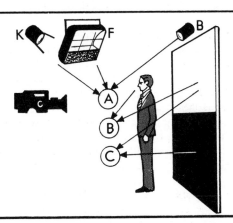

Light measurement
A Checking incident light levels – key, fill, back light
B Checking subject-to-background contrast, to ensure good tonal separation (e.g. 1½:1 or 2:1 typical)
C Checking the scene's tonal contrast (e.g. 20:1 max) to allow for lighting increasing contrast range further

Lighting and sound

The microphones used in video production can be supported in several different ways: worn or held by performers (*personal mikes*), clipped into vertical *floor stands*, *slung above the action*, fixed to a *fishpole*, or *suspended* in a *sound boom*.

How sound pickup affects lighting
Microphones below head-height pose no lighting hazards.

- A *slung* microphone may cast shadows onto faces and scenery, but careful lamp positioning and barndooring usually avoid this problem.
- A *fish pole* (*fishing rod*) simply consists of a mike at the end of a pole, which is pointed towards the sound source. It may inadvertently move into the key light's beam and throw shadows onto the speaker or the background; but difficulties are minimal.
- The *sound boom*. In smaller versions, a wheeled tripod with a central column, supports a centrally-pivoted horizontal tube (the *boom arm*). The microphone attached to one end of this tube is counterbalanced by a weight at the other. The operator moves the boom arm, and swivels/tilts the mike to follow the action. On larger sound booms, the arm-length can be continually adjusted to follow performers' movements.

The microphone is always kept outside the camera's field of view; placed around 0.6–1.8 m (2–6 ft) in front of the speaker, according to the size of the shot. Shadows of the mike and the boom arm can fall onto people and background, so care is needed in selecting the key's angle, and positioning the boom.

Controlling boom shadows
- *Is the mike shadow visible in shot?* Remember, there will always be a shadow from the boom mike if a hard key is used. Aim to throw it out of shot, or disguise it (e.g., hide it in a background shadow).
- *Can the mike be moved to avoid the shadow?* The mike's position should relate to the shot size; i.e., close for a close-up, distant for a long shot. Sometimes the mike can be raised or angled to clear the shadow.
- *Can the lighting be adjusted to clear or hide the shadow?* Often you can shade the background with a barndoor flap where the shadow appears, so 'hiding' it. But this may degrade the lighting treatment.
- *Can the lighting be planned to avoid shadows?* Normally shadows are thrown out of shot by placing the key on the opposite side of the camera to the boom, and using upstage or side-wall keys for cross-shooting cameras. Sometimes a different form of sound pickup (e.g., personal mike) is the only way of avoiding shadows.

AVOIDING SOUND BOOM SHADOWS

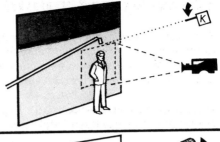

Barndoor
Lowering the top barndoor flap may shade off the area containing the sound boom shadow

Moving the key
Where the boom operator is unable to avoid a shadow, it may be necessary to move the key (from 1 to 2)

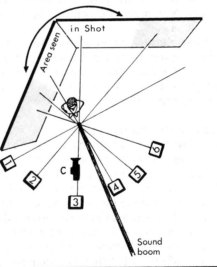

Anticipating the boom shadow
Here you see where boom shadows would fall for various key light positions. Keys 1 and 2 (on the opposite side of camera to the boom) are typical, and throw the shadow out of shot. Keyed from 3 or 4, shadows are unavoidable. 5 and 6 would avoid shadows, but are too widely angled for good portrait lighting

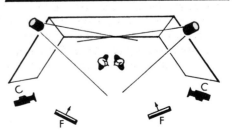

Upstage keys
When keys are located on the far side of action (upstage), boom shadows are generally cast forwards, and are not seen by cross-shooting camera

137

Picture control

Shooting with a single video camera one often relies on the camera's inbuilt automatic controls to adjust the picture quality: *Auto-iris* (exposure), white balance, auto black level, auto focus. . . . So it is possible to simply point and shoot, leaving the rest to electronics! Although this 'hands-off' approach to camerawork certainly produces results, they are not necessarily optimum.

Multi-camera units are cabled to a *camera control unit (CCU)/base station*. Here picture quality is continually monitored and adjusted by a separate operator – the *video engineer/'shader'/vision control operator*. This system provides the highest consistent picture quality, particularly when matching inter-cut shots.

Operational controls
The main controls are:

- *Exposure* – The camera can only handle a limited tonal range. Adjusting lens aperture allows you to select the range of scenic tones that is reproduced best: i.e., to adjust *exposure*. If lightest tones are over-light, or crush to white, stop the lens down (but darker tones become less visible). If modeling and detail is insufficient in darker tones, opening up the aperture will improve reproduction (but light tones will pale, and may block off/burn out to white). 'Correct exposure' can vary between shots, but good face tones are usually the governing factor.
- *Black level* – The camera's video signal is usually adjusted so that its darkest areas are reproduced as black. However, it is possible to 'set up/sit up' the entire video, so that all tones are reproduced proportionally lighter (without revealing further detail in shadows). This produces an overall high-key effect. Conversely, by 'setting down/ sitting down' the video waveform, darker tones can be merged to black; e.g., to create deep shadows, night effects, or to consolidate black backgrounds.
- *Gamma adjustments* – The 'gamma control' modifies the reproduced picture's tonal contrasts (its 'vigor', 'snap', 'bite') from a strongly contrasted harsh quality, to a thin subtly-graded effect. Gamma is often readjusted to improve shadow detail, or to show gradation more clearly in light-toned areas such as snow or plaster.
- *Color balance (white balance)* – The relative amplification (gain) of the camera's red, green, and blue channels, is normally adjusted to produce a neutral gray scale, with lighting of a particular color quality. If the color temperature of the light changes, or you want the picture to look warmer or cooler, the camera's color balance can be changed.

138

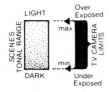

20:1 Tonal Contrast (or below)

EXPOSURE

The camera's tonal range
Most video systems can only reproduce a limited range of tones accurately. The lightest tone is about 20 to 30 times as bright as the darkest. For any tones beyond these limits, tonal gradation and detail are lost in the picture

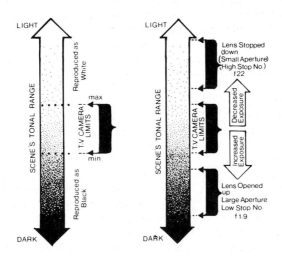

Adjusting exposure
The scene in front of the camera often contains a very wide range of tones; well beyond the camera's limits. (Tonal contrasts are deliberately restricted in the studio)

As you adjust the lens aperture, you are actually selecting which segment of the scene's complete tonal range you want to reproduce accurately. Flesh tones usually lie around the center of that range

139

Power supplies

You can power lamps from sources as diverse as belt batteries, car batteries, mobile generators, public utility supplies. The larger the fixtures, the greater the care needed in handling, supporting and powering them.

Power requirements
Many factors affect the amount of power you need for a production, including the design and efficiency of the equipment. For a given power consumption, fresnel spotlights provide a greater output than soft light sources. Metal-halide lamps have much higher outputs than equivalent tungsten bulbs. Any scrims/diffusers and color medium reduce the light output.

Techniques, too, will influence power needs; e.g., how much of a particular background appears in shot; the effect required; the number of lamps you use to light it, etc.

Power in the studio
Basically, the main power supply is split at a central *lighting board/ lighting console* into a series of identical power lines or *channels*. Each numbered channel has its own dimmer and on/off switch. All the cables from these supplies go to corresponding outlet sockets (receptacles) on a master *patch panel*.

Studio lamps are plugged into nearby outlets (on walls and overhead battens/barrels); which are permanently cabled to a series of numbered plugs at the patch panel.

So to power a lamp, you simply insert (*patch*) a *plug* which is cabled to a lamp, into a numbered power outlet from the central dimmer board.

Power on location
On location (and in some studios), the *main feeder cable* from the supply source runs to a master *distribution box* (*spider, plugging box*). Secondary feeder cables are plugged into this box to take power to a series of fused receptacles. Further *extension cables* then distribute power to individual or groups of lighting fixtures. Various types of *connections* are used on equipment and cables, each with particular advantages. The trick is to ensure that they all match! Both fusible links and cut-outs are used to prevent overload, and additional fuses may be fitted to individual lamps.

Light intensities are basically adjusted with scrims/diffusers and lamp adjustment. But where lighting changes are needed, a range of portable equipment is available, including switches or dimmers on individual lamp circuits, group switches (*contact breakers*), and small dimmer packs and control desks.

POWER CONSUMPTION TABLE

Power (watts)	110 V	120 V	220 V	240 V supply
100	0.9	0.8	0.5	0.42
150	1.4	1.3	0.7	0.63
200	1.8	1.7	0.9	0.83
375	3.4	3	1.7	1.6
500	4.5	4.2	2.3	2.1
650	6	5.4	3	2.7
800	7.3	6.7	3.6	3.3
1000	9	8.3	4.5	4.2
1250	11.3	10.4	5.7	5.2
1500	13.6	12.5	6.8	6.3
2000	18.2	16.7	9	8.3
5000	45.5	42	22.7	20.8
10,000	91	83	45.5	41.7

| Current | Power in watts | | | |
Amps	110	120	220	240 volts
5	550	600	1100	1200
10	1100	1200	2200	2400
13	1430	1560	2860	3120
15	1650	1800	3300	3600
20	2200	2400	4400	4800
25	2750	3000	5500	6000
30	3300	3600	6600	7200
40	4400	4800	8800	9600
50	5500	6000	11000	12000

Cable connections

Internationally, a wide range of connectors is used, of which the following are typical:

Household/domestic plugs (plastic or rubber).
USA 110/120 v maximum load 15 amp. No earthing (ground) 2-prong. Maximum load 2 kw.
British 220/240 v maximum load 13 amp. Fused. Earthed 3-pin. Maximum load 3 kw.
Heavy duty household. Maximum load 30 amp. Earthed (grounded) 3-prong.

Pin connector plugs. Small rectangular plastic block. 2 or 3 conductor pins on one side. For heavy duty cables. Location use. Tie cable ends together.

Stage plugs (floor plugs, Kliegl plugs). Rectangular cable plug ½ in/1 in wide has large flat sprung conductor on either edge. Rectangular heavy-duty metal distribution box (with 1–6 connector receptacles). Will accept several plugs side-by-side. Available in fused or earthed versions. Not color-coded. Supply polarity uncertain. Plug can be dislodged from receptacle, causing poor contact (surface-burning and over-heating).

Twist-lock plugs. Plug has three curved metal connectors (one earth) that lock firmly into slots in the socket receptacle, with ¼-turn twist.

Single-pin connectors. Separate heavy-duty thick metal pins (color-coded) fit into 3-receptacle sockets.

Technicolor lugs. Large slotted cylindrical copper molding with a securing screw, brazed or crimped onto cables, fixing onto bus bars (wide thick copper strip) of company supplies, distribution point/service panel (head).

Molded rubber plugs. Large molded rubber plugs with 3 connector pins (one earth), held by retaining skin in 1–4 way molded rubber receptacle (loads 1–10 kw).

Mareshal decontactor type DS. Special molded weatherproof metal fitting with nylon insert in ratings 30–500 A. Shuttered live contacts for five-pin arrangement.

Flat-blade connector (Tri Edison). In two forms: Central straight key blade (ground) and two 45° angled blades; U-shaped key (ground) and two parallel blades.

Safety

In a busy production, you are surrounded with potential 'accidents waiting to happen'. Preoccupied with the job in hand, it is all too easy to overlook these hazards. So here is a list of reminders you may find helpful.

General precautions – Make sure that lighting fixtures are secure, not liable to fall, twist or overbalance. Loops of steel wire (bonds, strops) on fixtures or accessories will prevent them from falling. Wire mesh guards can protect people from exploding light bulbs or broken lenses. Remember all lighting fixtures need good ventilation. Badly fitted scrims/diffusers or color medium, can cause units to overheat, and reduce lamp life. Keep fixtures well away from drapes, cyc, scenery (they can scrape, tear, cause surface damage, and are a fire risk when hot). Do not allow water spray to fall onto lamps, cables or connections. (Bulbs explode!) Prolong the life of lamps and fresnel lenses, by fading lamps up from cold, rather than switching on full power.

Cable care – Do not use cables partly coiled (they can overheat). When running out a cable do not pull it by a connector, avoid its becoming taut, knotted, trapped under heavy objects, or dragged over sharp edges. Keep the floor clear of cables where possible; sling, conceal, or cover them. Keep cables well away from hot fixtures, water, or damp ground. Protect cables from possible run-over by camera dollies, vehicles, etc. Always use lighting cables well within their rated limits. Protect cable connectors against damage or debris. Ensure that cables are firmly inter-connected (tie ends together if necessary to prevent pull-out).

Lighting stands – Take care not to overbalance lighting stands. Particularly when fully extended, bottom weighting is essential (using sand bags, stage weights). Secure the fixture's cable (clipped to the stand, weighted near the stand base) to prevent the stand from being displaced or overbalanced.

Hung fixtures (slung lamps) – Take particular care when raising/lowering lighting battens/barrels or fixtures. It is easy to inadvertently lower them onto people, scenery, furniture. If 'brail lines' (cord) are used to pull suspended lamps off-vertical, secure them well (they can slip or break) and avoid undue strain. Suspended lamps at around head height are a danger to people and to moving cameras/sound booms. Hang clear warning 'flags' on them.

Handling fixtures – Many fixtures are awkwardly balanced and heavy. Do not move lit lamps (hot filaments are fragile). Take particular care when operating or moving hot fixtures (wear heavy gloves). Use correct lifting techniques when lifting and carrying fixtures.

Ladders/treads/steps – Fully extend folding ladders/steps and set them down firmly on even flat ground. Have someone hold the ladder steady while working, and do not lean over to one side (it easily overbalances). Lower suspended fixtures by rope; don't carry them down the ladder. Never stand on the top rungs/treads. Fold and store units securely (do not leave them open or leaning against a wall).

142

Grounding/earthing – All equipment including lighting fixtures, practical lamps, electrical apparatus, scenic metalwork, supplies, should be properly *grounded*, to avoid electric shocks.

Phases – Electrical equipment fed from different supply phases, must be kept well apart to avoid shock due to voltage differences between them.

Fuses and circuit breakers – Check that these are rated to suit the current consumption of the units they supply, and check their condition periodically.

Equipment condition – Check cables for cable-fraying, chafing, splits, etc. Check grounding. Check lighting fixtures for damage, corrosion, rust, etc. Check that bulbs are securely seated, without undue blackening, blisters, distortion. Always switch lighting circuits off, and wait for fixtures to cool down, before changing lamps. Check the type of lamp before replacing it (the code is marked on its base). Clean reflectors periodically to avoid light losses; but take care not to get cleaner into lamp holder and mechanism.

Patching – Always switch circuits *off* before patching or depatching. Inserting or removing a plug from a 'live' ('hot') circuit causes arcing at contacts, burning and blackening them. Do not exceed dimmer ratings by patching too many lamps into a circuit (particularly when there are duplicate/multi-socket outlets available). Although you have checked the combined power of lamps plugged into a circuit, is there already an existing load on it?

Supplies – Where utility supplies are 120 volts a.c., wall outlets are rated for a maximum of 15 amps (i.e. 1800 watts) or 30 amps (3600 watt). For mains supplies of 240 volts a.c. wall points are 13 amps maximum (3120 watt). These are easily exceeded, especially when using extension cords. *AVOID* makeshift, improvised 'lash-ups', using temporary bindings round connections or damaged cables!

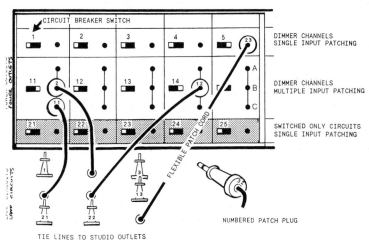

TIE LINES TO STUDIO OUTLETS

Take care when patching lamps
If you do not take care when patching, you can overload circuits, burn connections, and accidentally light studio lamps that are not in use!

143

Further reading

Carlson, V. and S.:
Professional Lighting Handbook
A description and discussion of the general hardware of film lighting.

Millerson, Gerald:
The Technique of Lighting for Television and Film
An internationally established sourcebook, discussing in detail the principles and techniques of the art of lighting.

Video Camera Techniques
A quick lucid guide to the essentials of handling video cameras.

TV Scenic Design Handbook
A study in depth of the art, the mechanics, and techniques of scenic design for television and video production.

Effective TV Production
A 'succinct but thorough overview of the production process' (American Cinematographer) distilled for rapid study into a single volume.

The Technique of Television Production (12th Edition)
A comprehensive encyclopedic study of the mechanics, techniques, and esthetics of television production.

Samuelson, David:
Motion Picture Camera and Lighting Equipment
Includes extremely useful data on film lighting equipment; much of which directly relates to video production.

Glossary

Acting area   The part of a setting/staging area in which the action/performance takes place.

Adapter   An accessory that allows one type of termination to be connected into another of different design, e.g. to interconnect different cable plugs and receptacles; or to match different sizes of spigots and sockets ('reducers').

Ambient light   General undirected lighting in an environment.

Ampere (amp; A)   Unit used to measure the amount of electric current passing through a circuit. It increases with the power of the load; and as the resistance (impedance) of the load is reduced. *See* **Watts, Volts**

Auto-transformer   An iron-cored coil across an a.c. power supply, that allows a variable voltage to be tapped off, so providing an adjustable supply to a lamp, and varying its brightness.

Automatic voltage control (automatic voltage regulation–AVR)   Circuitry for automatically adjusting the supply voltage, to keep it within prescribed limits as the lighting load varies. Without such control, the supply voltage may fall as groups of lamps are switched on (all lamps become dimmer, with a lower color temperature), and rise rapidly as some lamps are switched off (surge) – possibly burning out ('blowing') those that remain alight.

Available light   A general term for the existing light (natural or artificial) one finds when shooting on location. This may need to be modified or augmented for technical or artistic reasons, to suit the video system.

Back light   Light directed towards the camera, usually onto the rear of a subject in order to define its outline, model its edges, or reveal translucency.

Balance (of lighting)   Adjusting the relative intensities of the lamps lighting the subject and its surroundings, to create a particular artistic effect (atmosphere, time, mood, etc.).

Barndoors   A rotatable metal frame with two or four hinged flaps (two large, two smaller), that can be fitted to the front of a spotlight, to cut off parts of its light beam.

Barrel   A horizontal tubular steel bar (e.g. 1.2–2.7 m/4–9 ft long), suspended at each end, and used to support lighting fixtures. Its height may be adjusted using counter-balance weights, hand-cranked or motor-driven hoists. Power outlets are provided at its ends.

Base light (foundation light)   An even intensity soft light distributed over a setting to minimize lighting contrast and avoid exaggerating the reproduced tonal contrasts of the scene.

Batten   A long suspended lamp-support bar (e.g. 3–4.5 m/9–15 ft long). Power outlets are provided at intervals along its length. *Also* A stage lighting trough or strip light fixture.

Batting down on blacks   Adjusting the video signal to crush the darkest picture tones to an even black ('black crushing'; 'sitting hard').

Black level   The tonal level on the video waveform, below which the system reproduces all signals as black.

Blackout   To switch all lights out (or fade to a blank screen) for effect.

Bloom (block off, crush-out, burn-out)   When the brightest picture tones reach the upper limits of the video system (the 'white clipper'), they merge to become a blank white area. (Blooming usually arises through over-exposure, over-lighting, specular reflections. Also due to unsuitable surface finish, tone or angle.)

Break though   A spurious effect that can occur when electronically inserting a subject (chroma key). Parts of the background shot appear 'within' the subject; e.g. a blue neck-tie vanishes, and the background scene is visible there instead!

Bridge   A suspended tubular-scaffolding cradle or gangway, used to provide an operating position for a follow spot, or to support heavy lighting equipment.

Brightness (luminosity)   Our subjective impression of the amount of light reflected from surfaces. Often very inaccurate, due to psychological effects (adaption illusions); e.g., a pure (highly saturated) color may be wrongly interpreted as 'bright'.

Also, **brightness** is often used to denote *luminance* (the correct term for accurate measurements of reflected light).

Cameo   A type of presentation in which action takes place against a black background.

Camera left   Left-hand side of the picture (performers' right side; O/P side).

Camera light   A small lamp attached to the camera to provide local frontal fill light for close-ups, eyelights, or a traveling key light.

Camera right   Right-hand side of the picture (performers' left side; prompt side)

Camera trap   A limited opening provided within scenery, that allows a camera to shoot into the setting from otherwise inaccessible positions. Pull-aside drapes, shutters, hinged wall-pictures, sliding panels, etc., are used as camera traps.

Camera tube (pickup tube)   The camera lens image is focused onto a light sensitive *target* in the camera tube. Here charges build up corresponding with the light and shade in the image, and are rhythmically scanned in a series of lines to produce a continuous video signal.

Carbon arc   An electric arc created between two cerium-cored carbon rods, produces a high intensity gaseous discharge; creating a white light of excellent color quality. The small source creates sharply defined shadows. The carbon *trims* have a limited burning time (e.g. 45–90 minutes), and require skilled operation and maintenence to achieve an even, constant light output.

Catwalk   A walkway in the studio ceiling, above any lighting grid, giving access to suspended lighting and scenic equipment, air conditioning, hoists, etc. *Also* A narrow balcony (lighting gantry) fixed high around studio walls. Here lighting fixtures can be attached to tubular rails, cables and ropes secured, etc.

CCD (charge-coupled device)   A solid-state image sensor using a small silicon chip containing thousands of individual elements, each independently charged by light from corresponding parts of the lens image.

C-clamp   A molded C-shaped fitting which hangs from an overhead pipe/barrel/batten, and holds a lighting fixture in its lower socket.

Center stage   A position in the center of the acting area.

Channel monitor   A preview picture monitor which continuously displays the output of a particular camera, VTR, film channel, etc.

Cheat   To rearrange something from a previously established position (or lighting condition), hoping that the audience will not notice the alteration.

Chiaroscuro   The most familiar pictorial treatment, in which a three-dimensional illusion is created by lighting and staging. An impression of solidity and depth is achieved by tonal gradation, carefully related brightnesses of planes, tonal separation, and shadow formations.

Chroma   *See* **Saturation**.

Chroma key   Automatic electronic switching circuitry (self-keying), which relies on color differentiation to insert subjects from one video source into the corresponding part of another picture (background).

CID (compact iodide daylight) lamp   A type of gas-discharge lamp, available in single-ended bare bulb and PAR versions.

146

Color balance The adjustment of the relative strengths of the primaries of the color system (red, green, blue) to provide optimum color fidelity. When a system is accurately balanced throughout, each gray scale step (value) from white' down through grays to 'black', will appear neutral (i.e., without coloration). When this *gray-scale tracking* is correct, there will be no color cast.

Color correction filter (light conversion filter, color compensating filter) Color medium placed over a light source to modify its color quality; e.g., to match light of low color temperature (e.g., tungsten), to high color temperature illumination (e.g., daylight).

Color medium (gels) A colored transparent or translucent material (typically gelatin, acetate, polyester, acrylic sheet) placed in front of a lamp to color the emergent light.

Color temperature The color quality of light, theoretically relating its spectral distribution to that of a heated standard 'black body' radiator. Measured in degrees Kelvin, where $0°K = -273°C$. Each form of luminant tends to have its particular color quality: e.g., daylight 5600 K, tungsten-halogen lighting 3200 K. The effective color temperature can be altered by attaching a suitable correction filter to the light source or the camera lens. (Bluish filter raises the color temperature; yellowish-orange lowers it.) Such filters made of glass or gelatin are classified in *mireds*, and produce a color shift which depends on the original color temperature.

Contactor A remotely controlled heavy-duty relay, used to switch lamps connected to it.

Contrast range (subject brightness range) The brightness ratio between the lightest and darkest tones in a scene. *Also* The extreme ratio that a system can accommodate while still reproducing all intermediate tones reasonably accurately (30 : 1).

Contrast ratio A measurement of the relative 'brightness' of any two tones, given as a luminance ratio. Thus if a subject is twice as bright as its background, they would have a 2 : 1 contrast ratio.

Contrasty A picture with extreme tones, and few intermediate half tones (high gamma).

Cookie (cucaloris, cuke) An irregularly shaped or stencilled sheet placed in front of a spotlight either to produce uneven light intensities (light break-up) or a distinct shadow effect (dappling).

Cove (merging cove, ground cove) A low ramp with a concave or sloping surface, placed at the bottom of a cyclorama to hide where it joins the floor, and help to merge the two surfaces.

Cross fade Progressively fading one lamp out, while fading up another; usually so that the average light intensity remains reasonably constant (dipless fade).

Cross-shot A camera viewpoint that is oblique to the action area, as opposed to a *frontal* or *head-on shot*, in which the camera looks straight onto the scene.

CSI lamp (compact source iodide) Form of gas discharge source.

Cyan A blue-green hue. Minus red (i.e., white light minus its red component). Results from adding blue plus green light.

Cyc light A lighting fixture with a specially shaped reflector producing a broad elongated light beam, that enables a cyclorama (or other background) to be lit evenly overall from a relatively close distance.

Cyclorama (cyc) A vertical hung cloth (usually stretched) used as a general-purpose scenic background. May be arranged in a shallow 'C' form (*curved cyc*), or with a straight rear wall and straight sides at right angles (*wrapround cyc*).

Dead No longer required. *Also* When a suspended lighting fixture is raised/lowered/brailed over, its final position is its 'dead'.

Dichroic A glass light filter with a specially coated surface that restricts certain parts of the spectrum (through interference effects). Placed over a tungsten halogen lamp (3200 K), the effective color temperature of its light can be converted to 5600 K (daylight).

Diffuser (scrim) Translucent material attached to the front of a lighting fixture to disperse and soften the light quality, or to reduce its intensity. Spun-glass sheet and frosted plastic sheeting are widely used.

Dimmer truck A mobile wheeled box fitted with a series of resistance dimmers.

Dirty light If when lighting a background, adjacent light beams do not meet, the underlit area between them can appear on camera as a shadow area.

Dipping Lightly dyeing white or light-toned fabrics (e.g., to coffee or blue tints) to reduce blooming. Typically used on white shirts, sheets, table-covering, drapes, etc.

Doubling The result of two (or more) light sources illuminating the same area. Doubling can cause hotspots, multiple shadows, uneven coverage, but may be deliberate where a single source provides insufficient light intensity.

Downstage In video/TV production indicates 'nearer the camera'. Hence 'move downstage'.

Dual source lamp A lighting fixture that can be transformed from a 'soft' light source, to a 'hard' source. Usually incorporating two separate units fitted at either end of a box housing.

Dulling spray (anti-flare) A wax spray, used to diffuse and reduce shine (specular reflections) on glass, metal, polished surfaces. If excessive, the coating may alter the subject's appearance.

Ellipsoidal spotlight, profile spot, projection spotlight, effects spot) A spotlight in which light collected from an ellipsoidal mirror reflector is focused by a lens system, to project a hard-edged beam or a metal gobo pattern. Independent internal framing-shutters (blades) adjust the beam shape. An internal variable iris may adjust beam intensity.

Exposure The selective control of reproduced tonal values within a system's limits. Strictly, *over exposure* results when reflected light exceeds the camera's handling limits. *Under-exposure* when a surface is insufficiently bright to be clearly discerned in the picture. However a subject is often said to be 'over' or 'under' exposed when it appears brighter or darker in the picture than is artistically desirable – even where tones lie well within the system's range. Exposure can be controlled by adjustment of the lens aperture, light intensities, neutral density filters.

Fill light (filler, fill-in) Diffused light used to illuminate shadow areas and reduce lighting contrast, without casting further shadows.

Flag A metal plate fixed in an adjustable angle-arm support, held in a light beam to provide a shadow (hard or soft edged), or to keep light off a selected area.

Fluorescent lamp A tubular lamp in which a mercury-vapor discharge energizes a fluorescent powder that coats the inside of the tube. Because its light quality has pronounced spectral peaks, it does not directly relate to Kelvin color quality standards. Instead, tubes have *correlated color temperature* ratings (e.g. 3000 K, 4800 K 6500 K).

Gaffer grip ('gator grip) A clip fitting (sprung or screw adjusted) incorporating a support spigot which enables a lightweight lamp to be attached to a structure (e.g., door, chair, pipe, pole).

Gaffer tape A wide plasticized-fabric adhesive tape with many productional uses: to fix lightweight lamps to walls secure cables, etc., to mark floor positions (floor marks) for performers, lamps, furniture.

148

Gamma A measurement of tonal gradation in reproduction. A *high gamma* picture has few half-tones (i.e., tends to 'soot and whitewash'). A *low gamma* picture clearly reproduces gray-scale differences over a narrower contrast range. Unless the overall gamma of a system is unity, relative tonal and color values are reproduced inaccurately.

Gantry A walkway around the upper part of studio wall, with support rails for heavy lighting fixtures (follow spot, carbon arcs). Also giving access to tying-off points for suspended scenery, lighting and sound outlets.

Gobo A jet-black screen (wooden, cloth) used to hide lamps or cameras from certain viewpoints. *Also* A large flag, used to shield light from an area. *Also* A small metal stencil used to project light patterns.

Grid In large studios, a framework 'floor' fitted over the staging area, near the studio roof. Walkways (catwalks) give access to lighting and scenic hoists, lighting suspension fittings (monopoles), ventilation, etc. *Also* In small studios, a permanent *pipe grid* (lattice of tubular piping) is fixed just below the ceiling, to which lighting fixtures are attached with *C-clamps*.

Groundrow A series of lighting fixtures laid on the floor (often behind low scenic flats, coves, etc.,) to illuminate a background – troughs, battens, cyc lights. *Also* Term for a low horizontal scenic plane, often representing distant landscape, city skyline.

Hanger A suspended vertical support tube, of fixed or adjustable length, from which a lighting fixture is hung; a 'drop arm'. (Also used generally for all lighting suspension devices, including *pantographs*.)

Hertz (Hz) Unit used to measure the frequency of alternating current, in cycles per second. (One complete oscillation equals one cycle; i.e., 1 hertz.)

High key A picture in which mid to light tones predominate, with little or no shadow.

HMI lamp (hydrargyrum medium arc-length iodide) A mercury-halide lamp in tubular, double-ended form. Available in ratings up to 18 kW. Correlated color temperature of 5600 K or 3200 K.

Hoist A remotely-winched or motor-driven mechanism controlling a wire cable hanging from the ceiling. Used to suspend or support lighting equipment, and/or scenery, slung picture monitors, cables, etc.

House lights Powerful ceiling lights used to illuminate the studio overall as a general 'working light' (e.g., for rigging, setting scenery, etc.,). House lights are extinguished when the production lighting equipment is in use.

Hue The predominant sensation of color; i.e., red, green, blue, etc.

Key light The main light illuminating a subject – usually a fresnel spotlight. The key light reveals the subject's form, contours, texture, and may suggest the prevailing light direction (e.g., that sun is coming from a nearby window).

Kilowatt (kW) One thousand watts.

Lag (trailing) A smearing after-image following a moving object (persistence).

Lamp A general term for a *lighting fixture* (*luminaire, lantern*). *Also* An incandescent light source (bulb, 'bubble').

Lens axis An imaginary line from the middle of a lens to the center of the shot.

Lens spot A spotlight in which light reflected from a mirror (often parabolic) is focused by a single-lens system. The distance between the lamp/reflector assembly and the lens is adjusted to alter the spotlight's beam angle (spread).

Lighting fixture An enclosure housing a lamp, reflector (mirror), and any associated lens system. Frequently simply called a 'lamp'.

Lighting ladders Wheeled ladder assemblies with safety rails and platform, used for rigging/adjusting hung lighting fixtures.

149

Lighting ratio   The ratio of 'key plus fill light' to the 'fill light' level.

Lighting stand   A telescopic vertical concentric tube with three horizontal bottom supports (legs). It has a tubular socket at its top, for a lamp spigot (16 mm/⅝ in. or 28 mm/1⅛ in. dia.).

Light levels   Intensity of illumination falling on (or reflected from) a scene, in lux or foot candles.

Lightness   The perceived brightness of surface color.

Light units   Standard methods of light measurement:

> *Incident light intensity* – Measured in *lux (lx)* or *foot candles (fc)*.
> *Reflected light intensity (surface brightness)* – *Nits (nt) (candela per sq m)* or *foot lamberts (ft/L) (candela per sq ft)*.
> *Color temperature* – Color quality of light measured in *Kelvins (K)*.
> *Light source strength* – *Lumens (lm), candela (cd)* or *candles*.
> *Hue* – *Nanometers, angstroms (A)* or *millimicrons*.

Limbo   A type of presentation in which action takes place against a white background.

Low key   A picture in which mid to lowest tones predominate, with few highlight details.

Luminance   Measurement of the true (not subjective) brightness of a surface. Doubling the illumination falling onto a surface, doubles its luminance; although to the eye, its apparent brightness only increases slightly. Snow has a high luminance, black velvet extremely low luminance. (Both are color-free neutrals, with zero saturation.)

Luminosity   The perceived brightness of light sources.

Magenta   A blue-red hue. Minus green (i.e., white light minus its green component). Results from adding blue plus red light.

Matching   Maintaining visual continuity between consecutive pictures, to ensure that they have compatible brightness, contrast, light direction, color quality, etc.

Metal-halide discharge lamps   A gas discharge light source comprising two metal electrodes in a suitable gas vapor (mercury vapor, argon gas) with metallic iodides (rare earths) which increase the source's spectral spread and improve its color quality. Highly efficient, it may use ⅓ to ⅕ the power of an equivalent tungsten-halogen lamp. However, it takes a 'warm-up' period on switch-on to reach full output (± 3 minutes) and a 'recovery period' before re-lighting (10–15 minutes). The source requires an *ignitor/ballast unit* to ignite the arc, and control current flow. Types of metal-halide discharge lamp include HMI, CSI and CID lamps.

Mireds (micro reciprocal degrees)   Units used to relate or compare color temperatures, especially when selecting compensatory filters. (One mired equals a million divided by kelvins; thus 5000 K = 200 mireds.)

Monochrome   Strictly speaking, 'single color'. Usually refers to 'black-and-white' picture reproduction.

Munsell system   A system of color notation, that classifies a wide range of hues for varying degrees of saturation.

Neutral density filter   A neutral-toned filter material of specified density that absorbs light equally over the spectrum; so reduces light intensity without affecting its color quality.

Nook light   A small open fronted trough fitting, containing a short strip-light (tubular lamp) with a curved rear reflector. This lightweight source can be attached by tape or gaffer-grip to most surfaces. The light quality is fairly hard, but can be used to fill local shadow areas.

150

Notan A pictorial style that is mainly concerned with surface detail, color and outline, rather than an illusion of solidity and depth.

Off stage A position outside the acting area. To move 'off-stage' is to move away from the center of the acting area.

On stage A position near the center of the acting area.

Overload To exceed the handling capacity of the system. In lighting, an excess power demand relative to a cable or supply's current or wattage rating, causing heating in wiring, connectors, etc., and voltage losses. Excess current causes safety devices (fuse, contact breaker) to operate, and disconnect the supply.

Pantograph A form of lighting hanger based on lazy-tongs principle. Available in single and double form. Strip springs counterbalance the weight of attached lighting fixtures, and allow lamp height to be adjusted easily over a wide range.

PAR lamp A tungsten-halogen lamp, in which the inside of the bulb provides a *parabolic aluminized reflector*. This together with the molded glass front (plain, ribbed, or lens) provides a fixed beam-spread with wide, medium or medium coverage. A blue filter for daylight correction may be incorporated, or clipped on. PAR lights are used individually, or grouped in floodlight banks.

Patching Each studio lamp plugs into a wall-outlet socket attached to a supply line. This line normally terminates in a *patch-cord*, which can be plugged into any of a series of independently numbered supply circuits in a *patchboard (patch panel)*. Each power circuit has its associated dimmer and switch control circuit.

Pea light (pea lamp, Christmas tree light) A tiny lamp used for decorative effects, e.g., to simulate stars.

Phase Industrial electrical power is supplied as a *three-phase* alternating current (a.c.) system. The three incoming phases (of identical voltage, but differing timing) are separated and distributed within a building. Studio lighting equipment requires *single-phase* supplies. Because a high voltage, exceeding the line supply, exists *between* the phases, it is essential that neighboring equipment be fed from the same phase supply, to avoid electric shocks.

Picture tube The cathode ray tube (CRT) in a TV monitor or receiver, containing the screen on which the picture is displayed.

Plate A metal plate fitted with a spigot or socket lamp support containing a socket, which can be screwed, hung, or taped to walls. A *profile* plate has a stepped cut-out which can be hung on vertical pipes.

Platform (parallel, rostrum) Demountable scenic unit, used to form raised flooring of various heights.

Plumbicon A lead-oxide camera tube widely used in video/TV cameras.

Pole, lighting (lighting hook) An extensible pole with an end fitting (hook or cup) enabling a suspended lighting fixture to be controlled from below at floor level (3–6 m/10–20 ft away). Adjustments include focus, tilt, pan, barndoors, source switching (hard/soft), power selection. (Colors identify the lamp controls.) This technique reduces the need for lighting ladders.

Power rail A ceiling track into which suspended lighting fixtures can be hooked or slotted, to provide power pick-up without individual lamp cabling.

Practical lamps Decorative or environmental light fittings arranged within a setting; e.g., table lamps. They may be *practical* (working) or *non-practical* (not working; i.e., decorative only).

Quartz halogen (quartz iodine) Tungsten halogen lamp. Quartz bulb filled with halogen gas.

Reflector spotlight A spotlight incorporating a simple parabolic mirror reflector (but no lens). Its beam angle is adjusted by altering the lamp-to-mirror distance. Widely termed 'external reflector, lensless', or 'open-bulb' spotlight.

Rig To install and set up lighting fixtures in their required positions. The finished assembly of lamps, positioned and patched for production.

Safety bond A clip-on wire strop or metal clip attached to equipment, to ensure that accessories cannot become detached, or fall off.

Sand bag A small sand-filled canvas bag used to weigh down lighting stands, cables, scenic supports, etc.

Saturation (chroma, intensity, purity) The purity of color. As a hue becomes paled-off or diluted by the addition of white light, it becomes *de*saturated.

SCR dimmer (silicon-controlled rectifier, thyristor) A solid-state electronic device used to control lamp brightness, by cutting off part of the cycle of its alternating current supply. (Design care is needed to prevent noise from lamps (lamp sing), or interference in the audio system.)

Scrim Stainless steel wire mesh used to control intensity. (Term often used for a *diffuser*.) *Also* Scenic gauze.

Sealed-beam lamp A tungsten lamp (normal or overrun filament) with a specially shaped internally-silvered bulb that serves as a reflector.

Seamless paper Tough paper (in rolls e.g., 2.7 m/9 ft wide and 11 m/36 ft long) used to form backgrounds or paper cycs. The brightness of its smooth surface is liable to vary with lighting and camera angles, particularly for darker tones.

Shutters A manually or remotely-adjusted metal venetian-blind placed in front of a light source to adjust the effective light output. (Color temperature remains constant.) Particularly used with non-dimmable carbon arcs, HMI arcs.

Silhouette A pictorial style which concentrates on subject outline for its effect. Surface detail, tone, color and texture are suppressed.

Simultaneous contrast (spatial induction) An illusion causing the apparent tone or hue of a subject to be influenced by its immediate background. Tones look lighter against a dark background, and darker against a light-toned background.

Space light A bare lamp surrounded by a skirt of white netting. Used overhead as an overall soft light (e.g., for 'open-air' scenes in the studio).

Specular reflections Highly intense reflections of lamps in shiny surfaces such as metal, glass, plastics, polished wood, gloss paint, etc. They reproduce as blank white areas. As well as being distracting, such highlights can become 'stuck-on' to the target of certain types of camera tubes (temporarily or permanently).

Spill light (fresh light, leak light) Uncontrolled light causing spurious patches, streaks, etc., on nearby surfaces.

Spill rings A series of shallow concentric cylinders fitted to the front of a light source to reduce light spread. (A lattice of close vertical and horizontal slats serves a similar purpose – *'eggcrate'*.)

Stage weight (brace weight) A cast-iron weight with a central hand grip, used to weigh down scenic supports, scenic units, and floor lighting equipment (e.g., extended lighting stands).

Staging The overall arrangement of scenic treatment within a studio.

Step lens A spotlight lens molded in a series of stepped concentric rings.

Support pole tubes ('Jack tubes, polecats, varipoles, barricudas, Acrows') Concentric spring-loaded tubes that wedge between ceiling and floor, or wall-to-wall (cross-tubes), to support lightweight lamps.

Surface brightness The amount of light reflected from a surface. It is affected by: the surface's *reflectance* (i.e., proportion of incident light reflected), the surface finish (rough, smooth), incident light intensity, the relative light and camera angles (brightness falls as either are angled), and the relative colors of the surface and light.

152

Throw The distance between a lamp and its destination. Hence a 'long throw' for a distant lamp, and a 'short throw' for a close lamp.

Trimming General term for the adjustment of a light source's exact coverage and intensity to produce the required artistic effect (*rough trim*, and *fine trim*).

Tungsten-halogen lamp/TH lamp/quartz light A type of tungsten lamp with improved performance; higher light output, almost constant output and color temperature, throughout a longer working life. These features are due to its halogen vapor filling (e.g., bromine, iodine). A recycling action causes tungsten evaporating from the filament to return to it, instead of being deposited as a black coating on the bulb as in regular tungsten lamps. Do not handle the quartz bulb; body acids attack its surface.

Tungsten lamp The familiar 'light bulb' in which a coiled tungsten-wire filament heats as an electric current passes through it. In use its filament gradually evaporates (black deposit), and the light output and color temperature fall.

Twin filament lamp A lamp with two separate filaments within the same bulb (envelope). Switching to single or double filaments, provides half or full power output. This allows overall light intensity to be altered without the use of dimmers (which would alter the color temperature).

Umbrella reflector A collapsible umbrella with a silvered or white interior, reflects light from a lamp attached to its handle. The resulting bounce light is very diffuse – but uncontrollable.

Underlighting Insufficient illumination relative to the required exposure and lighting balance (underlit conditions). *Also* Lighting directed up from below, usually for horrific or highly dramatic effects. Or more subtly, to reduce modeling/shadows from steep lighting.

Upstage Strictly, a position towards the back wall of a setting. *Also* Loosely, to indicate a position further from the camera (hence 'move upstage' i.e., away from the camera).

Value The subjective brightness of a surface (Munsell).

Video control (shading; vision control) Continual adjustment of camera channels to provide optimum picture quality and matching while shooting. Typical adjustments include exposure, black level (set-up, sit, lift), video gain, gamma, color balance.

Video noise (snow) Spurious background scintillations visible throughout the picture, but most obvious in darker tones. Due to weak video signal. (The video equivalent of photographic grain, tape hiss, disc surface noise).

Volt Unit of electrical pressure. A difference in potential at the supply, causes current to flow in a circuit. A circuit requires two supply lines. In a d.c. supply (e.g. a battery) one line is always positive, the other negative. The lines in an a.c. (alternative current) supply rhythmically fluctuate 60 (or 50) times a second (cycles), from positive to negative. It is essential that equipment is fed from appropriate supplies; i.e., the correct voltage, and a.c. or d.c.

Watt Unit of electrical power. It indicates the power consumed by electrical equipment. The energy may take the form of heat, light, or electromotive force. The greater the wattage rating, the higher the current flow. (1 kilowatt (1kW) equals 1000 watts.)

Wattage = *Current* times *voltage*.
Current = *wattage* divided by *voltage*.

Window filter Rigid acrylic sheet tinted orange (Wratten 85), fixed over windows to convert the daylight to a lower color temperature (e.g., 3200 K).

Xenon lamp A compact source discharge lamp containing xenon gas. This high intensity source has good color quality (6500 K), and is primarily used in projection equipment.

Yoke A 'square-U' shaped tubular frame, into which a lamp head is fitted, enabling it to tilt up/down. A *spud/spigot* (short metal rod or stud) in the center of the yoke fits into a tubular socket in a C-clamp, or the top of a lighting stand.